KNOW BULL'S
NO BULL
GUIDE TO
CITIZENSHIP

CELERA (CRA)

Edited by Achal Mehra

FROM THOSE WHO KNOW BULL
FOR THOSE WHO WOULD RATHER NOT

NOBLE PUBLISHERS
READING, PA

No Bull Guide to Citizenship

Book Editor
Achal Mehra

Series Editor
Achal Mehra

Cover Design
Shilpi Studios

Noble Publishers
101 North 5th Street
Berkshire Building, Suite 310
Reading, PA 19601
Tel: (610) 396-0194
Fax: (610) 396-0367
eMail: knowsbull@aol.com
Home Page: www.littleindia.com

Noble Publishers is a division of Little India

KNOW BULL'S
NO BULL GUIDES

Library of Congress Cataloging-in Publication Data
Mehra, Achal
   Know Bull's No Bull Guide to Citizenship
   1. Citizenship—United States—Handbooks, manuals.
   2. Naturalization—United States—Handbooks, manuals.
   3. Civics—Popular works.   I. Title

                                                    98-68355
   ISBN: 1-893333-04-3   CIP

Table of Contents

CHAPTER 1

In the Shadows of Citizenship

All children born in the United States, even those born to temporary visitors and illegal aliens, are U.S. citizens. Only children of foreign diplomats with full diplomatic immunity do not acquire U.S. citizenship by birth in the United States. Children born abroad to U.S. citizens also automatically acquire U.S. citizenship. This form of "natural born" citizenship is vested at and by birth. Another method of acquiring U.S. citizenship is through naturalization of permanent residents, which is an administrative process, administered by the Immigration & Naturalization Service (INS).

There are few legal distinctions between "natural born" and naturalized citizens. Naturalized citizens may not serve as president or vice president. They may run for the House of Representatives only after they have been citizens for seven years and for Senate only after nine years. Even though it is rare and difficult, the citizenship of naturalized citizens can be revoked, which is not possible for natural born citizens, unless they abandon their citizenship voluntarily.

Of the nearly 10.5 million legal permanent residents living in the United States, almost half, or 5.8 million, are eligible to apply for U.S. citizenship. The five million who are not eligible have yet to meet the residency requirements, which are typically five years for most permanent residents and three years for spouses of U.S. citizens. Table 1 provides a breakdown of permanent residents eligible for citizenship by state.

The past three years have witnessed a spurt in new citizenship applications, driven partly by political concerns over the denial of various welfare benefits and other social services to noncitizens. The number of citizenship applications quadrupled between 1992 and 1997 to 1.6 million. But applications dwindled to under a million in 1998. The recent decline in new citi-

Table 1
Permanent Residents Eligible for Citizenship

State	Permanent Residents	Eligible for Naturalization
Alabama	23,000	12,900
Alaska	10,900	4,800
Arizona	144,000	84,000
Arkansas	12,300	7,100
California	3,717,000	2,265,000
Colorado	71,000	38,000
Connecticut	126,000	73,000
Delaware	10,000	4,700
District of Columbia	42,000	23,000
Florida	790,000	405,000
Georgia	102,000	51,000
Hawaii	66,000	23,000
Idaho	16,000	9,800
Illinois	457,000	194,000
Indiana	46,000	28,000
Iowa	27,000	15,000
Kansas	36,000	22,000
Kentucky	21,000	11,500
Louisiana	47,000	27,000
Maine	14,700	10,000
Maryland	178,000	97,000
Massachusetts	310,000	177,000
Michigan	164,000	94,000
Minnesota	77,000	40,000
Mississippi	10,800	6,500
Missouri	44,000	23,000

State	Permanent Residents	Eligible for Naturalization
Montana	5,900	3,400
Nebraska	13,700	5,900
Nevada	53,000	33,000
New Hampshire	19,000	12,400
New Jersey	462,000	231,000
New Mexico	43,000	30,000
New York	1,498,000	669,000
North Carolina	64,000	35,000
North Dakota	4,900	2,200
Ohio	113,000	65,000
Oklahoma	32,000	18,000
Oregon	78,000	47,000
Pennsylvania	160,000	72,000
Rhode Island	47,000	31,000
South Carolina	24,000	13,400
South Dakota	4,400	1,900
Tennessee	37,000	20,000
Texas	825,000	483,000
Utah	33,000	19,000
Vermont	7,400	4,000
Virginia	183,000	97,000
Washington	174,000	84,000
West Virginia	7,000	3,800
Wisconsin	70,000	46,000
Wyoming	3,600	2,300
All U.S.	10,525,000	5,776,000

Source: Immigration and Naturalization Service. Column 2 is the number of permanent residents by state and Column 3 is the number eligible to apply for naturalization.

zenship applications is partly because some of the political threats to aliens have receded and also because many prospective citizens have become frustrated by INS delays, which are currently forcing most applicants to wait upwards of two years for their citizenship.

The citizenship application process is cause for needless anxiety among the hundreds of thousands of immigrants who apply for it annually. Between 1981-1990, the INS denied fewer than 2 percent of all petitions that were filed. During the past decade the denials have inched up somewhat, but even so fewer than 6 percent of naturalization petitions are denied by the INS. The odds are thus very much in your favor, so much of the anxiety surrounding the citizenship process is misplaced.

The citizenship process is neither arbitrary nor discretionary in the way that visa applications, for instance, can be at U.S. consulates. There are specific eligibility requirements that Congress has established and if you meet these naturalization conditions there is no reason to fear that your application will be declined.

The objective of this No Bull Guide to Citizenship is to demystify naturalization and to systematically walk you through the steps involved in filing your naturalization application. In the following chapters you will find hard nosed, no bull information on:

- Why you might want U.S. citizenship — and why you might not.
- Requirements for eligibility.
- Reasons for disqualification.
- Step-by-step completion of naturalization forms.
- Red flags: The areas you need to be cautious about.
- The INS Citizenship Test: Complete list of 100 questions with answers.
- The simpler 65/20 Citizenship Test for people over 65.
- The language requirements.
- The INS interview.
- The citizenship oath and ceremony.
- Dual citizenship: Can you retain your current citizenship after you take out U.S. citizenship?
- List of countries that allow dual nationality.
- The application checklist.
- Citizenship for children and veterans.

CHAPTER 2
_____

Why Citizenship?

Permanent residents, no matter how long they live or intend to live in the United States, need never become U.S. citizens. To be eligible for citizenship, permanent residents must meet the residency requirement, which is typically five years for most people. Spouses and some other narrow classes become eligible in just three years. Nearly half of all permanent residents presently do not meet that requirement and therefore are not eligible for citizenship until they have lived in the United States as permanent residents for the required period of five — or three — years.

The principal reason millions of eligible permanent residents chose not to take out citizenship is because doing so would require them to relinquish the citizenship of their home country (although this may not necessarily always result, see Chapter 8 on Dual Nationality). But there are also other considerations. This chapter explores the pros and cons of U.S. citizenship.

Benefits of citizenship

Citizenship confers many rights and privileges that are unavailable to aliens, including the right to vote, the ability to speed up or petition for the immigration of siblings, protection against deportation, exclusion from government benefits, the right to a U.S. passport and the services of U.S. embassies and consulates overseas.

Right to participate in the political process

Citizenship brings with it the basic democratic right to vote in elections as well as to run for office. In the wake of recent campaign finance scandals involving foreign contributors in U.S. elections, Congress has begun toying with legislation that would prohibit financial contributions by noncitizens to political candidates. Noncitizens who wish to get involved in the U.S. political process may find that the most expedient and effective way for them to do so is by taking out citizenship.

Ability to petition for relatives

Many immigrants desire to facilitate immigration to the United States by relatives. Citizenship helps them do so both by speeding up the process for some relatives and by making immigration possible for other categories of relatives, who they are unable to sponsor as permanent residents.

Permanent residents can petition only on behalf of spouses and *unmarried* children of any age. Citizens, on the other hand, can also file petitions on behalf of their married children, brothers and sisters, as well as parents. Thus citizenship may enable you to sponsor certain categories of relatives you are unable to sponsor as a permanent resident.

Furthermore, the processing time for the applications of relatives you are able to sponsor as a permanent resident is considerably higher than for citizens. Thus there is no waiting period for spouses of citizens since they are exempt from numerical quotas. By contrast, there is a waiting period of more than four years for spouses of permanent residents. Likewise, unmarried children of permanent residents have to wait for more than seven years for their visa, whereas such children of citizens have a waiting period of just a year. A permanent resident who might have to wait for four years for reunification with a spouse may be able to take out citizenship and bring the spouse over to the United States far more speedily. Table 2 lists the visa eligibility dates for various categories of family-sponsored preferences as of December 1998.

The U.S. passport

As a U.S. citizen you have the right to the U.S. passport, which allows you to travel for any length of time outside the United States without fear of forfeiting your legal residence status. As a permanent resident you are at risk of losing your permanent residence if you are outside the United States for more than a year at a time, unless you have secured prior approval from the INS. Ironically, U.S. citizenship may be most important for those who foresee that they may not be residing in the United States for long stretches of time, but wish to retain their U.S. ties either to be able to return to the United States or, as will be seen later, to preserve their social security, Medicare and other benefits if they elect to live abroad.

The U.S. passport also eases visa restrictions for travel to many coun-

Table 2

Visa Availability Dates for Family Preference Visas (December 1998)

Family	All Areas	China	India	Mexico	Philippines
1st Unmarried sons/daughters of U.S. citizens	15 Aug 97	15 Aug 97	15 Aug 97	1 Aug 93	1 April 87
2A Spouses/children of permanent residents	15 May 94	15 May 94	15 May 94	8 May 93	15 May 94
2B Unmarried adult sons/daughters of permanent residents	1 Mar 92	1 Mar 92	1 Mar 92	8 July 91	1 Mar 92
3rd Married adult sons/daughters of citizens	8 May 95	8 May 95	8 May 95	22 Mar 90	15 Mar 87
4th Brothers/sisters of U.S. citizens	22 April 88	22 April 88	1 May 86	8 Oct 87	1 Aug 78

Source: U.S. Department of State. Only applicants with priority dates earlier than the cut-off date listed here for their country may be be allotted a visa number. In effect, that means, these dates reflect the waiting period for allotment of their visa as of December 1998.

tries that are deferential to U.S. citizens. This is not uniformly true, however. The issue of admission to any country is obviously dependent on the laws of that country and its relationship with your home country. Generous bilateral or multilateral agreements among some countries may work to your advantage presently. Thus European countries facilitate travel among citizens of member European states, as do many Commonwealth countries.

If your travels are predominantly to a handful of countries, it may be worthwhile for you to explore with their embassies or consulates the visa requirements for both your current nationality and those for U.S. citizens. In addition, you need to consider that unless your home country allows dual nationality (see Chapter 8), you will no longer be able to use your current passport and will be treated as a foreign citizen by your home country.

You should check with your embassy or consulate on the travel and visa requirements for U.S. citizens as well as any special dispensation for its former citizens. India, for instance, has special rules for former Indian citizens, who are treated by law as people of Indian origin, with preferences in visa and investment matters that are not available to other foreigners. If your country permits dual citizenship, many of your current rights and privileges may be unaffected.

The U.S. passport also brings with it the benefit of U.S. government protection while you are overseas. If you need assistance while travelling abroad, you will be able to turn to U.S. embassies and consulates for services and support. Be mindful, however, that U.S. citizens are also the most visible target overseas and are at enhanced risk of terrorism than perhaps the citizens of virtually any other country.

Protection against deportation

A permanent resident can be deported for a wide range of reasons and even denied reentry into the United States. Over the past few years, Congress has been adding to the list of deportable offenses. Nearly 10,000 permanent residents are deported or expelled for various criminal and narcotic violations annually. Deportation may not only permanently bar you from the United States, it could also result in the loss of benefits, like social security.

A citizen is protected against such deportation. Even though there is a procedure for denaturalization, it is for the most part limited to activities in the pre-naturalization period, such as, for instance, lying in the naturalization application. Denaturalization is an extreme and rarely invoked penalty, permissible only if it was "illegally procured" or "procured by concealment of a material fact or by willful misrepresentation." It is exceedingly difficult and rare to denaturalize a citizen. Only 32 people were denaturalized in 1995, all because they had secured naturalization unlawfully through false statements in their naturalization applications.

Government benefits

Only citizens are eligible for certain public benefits and in recent years Congress has been adopting legislation to deny even more benefits to noncitizens. The Welfare Reform Act of 1996 bars legal permanent residents from many public benefits. In fact, the act, which is expected to save the federal government almost $56 billion, largely does so by denying many public benefits to noncitizens. Permanent residents who have not worked for at least ten years are barred from receiving food stamps and Supplemental Social Security Income (SSI) and other means-tested benefits. Although permanent residents presently receive social security and Medicare benefits, as both these funds become more vulnerable in future years, there is risk that noncitizens could face the paring knife first. Social security and Medicare reforms are high on the agenda of both political parties and major changes in both are highly likely in the next few years.

In addition, a permanent resident who accepts public benefits runs the risk of being found a public charge and excluded on reentry or even deported, although in practice that is rarely enforced. Permanent residents who live outside the United States for a period of over a year run the risk of losing their permanent residence status. The loss of permanent residence can, in turn, affect your eligibility for social security. Although, citizens of most countries continue to receive social security benefits to which they are eligible even if they abandon permanent residency in the United States, aliens from some countries can lose their benefits after six months. In addition, the social security administration withholds nearly 25 percent of the benefit payments of nonresident aliens as federal tax, which is not done with the payments of U.S. citizens living abroad. Areas of concerns can also arise for noncitizens through state actions. In many states, citizenship is a requirement for some state benefits.

Employment

Blanket bans on employment of aliens have been invalidated by the U.S. Supreme Court. However, the Court has permitted restrictions on alien employment in law enforcement, public schools and the federal civil service. Permanent residents who desire employment in these sectors may need to consider securing citizenship.

The risks of naturalization

Just as there are compelling considerations why you might want citizenship, there are also factors that you might want to weigh for passing up on U.S. citizenship as well. These include the possible loss of your current citizenship, as well as the potential risk of deportation in the case of denial of your citizenship application.

Loss of current citizenship

The single most important reason that many eligible permanent residents don't take out U.S. citizenship is because it would result in losing their current citizenship. Unless your home country recognizes dual nationality (See Chapter 8 on Dual Nationality to determine if you will retain or lose your current nationality after naturalization), you will lose your current citizenship when you naturalize. You may thus be compromising any future plans you might have of living or retiring in your homeland. Many countries offer generous travel and residency privileges to their former citizens, which might be adequate for your purposes.

You should investigate the consequences of losing your current citizenship on your current and future interests. Be mindful especially of economic policies. If you own property or stock equity, then abandoning your citizenship could potentially place such property at risk. Countries have very different policies on foreign ownership and some of them (such as India, which has a classification of person of Indian origin for tax and property purposes) may differentiate between foreigners and former citizens who originate from the country.

Unless you are able to maintain your original citizenship if your country permits dual nationality, you should be aware that your political and economic rights and obligations in virtually all countries change if you are not a citizen. If you have property interests of value, you should consider the consequences of abandoning your current citizenship to those interests. Your embassy or consulate is the obvious place to turn for answers to these questions. You may be able to structure your financial interests with your family and kin in a way that the negative impact on your finances is minimized.

In addition, as is discussed in Chapter 8, there may be disadvantages if your country treats you as a dual national, since you may be subject to the conflicting laws of two countries.

Risk of denial

The naturalization process is far more rigorous than the admission to permanent residence status and involves the investigation of your background and past. After an application for naturalization is filed, the INS examines whether the original acquisition of permanent residence was lawful, as well as whether the applicant may have become ineligible since. INS operating instructions require examiners to refer cases of potentially deportable aliens for consideration for initiation of deportation proceedings.

If there is something in your background, most notably if you have had brushes with the law, you run the risk not only of being denied citizenship, but also of losing your permanent residence status and deportation. The areas of particular concern are in the eligibility section of the form and are discussed in Chapters 3 and 4.

If you have concerns in any of these areas, you should either consult an attorney or reconsider the wisdom of applying for citizenship. Not all eligibility factors are grounds for deportation and you may not necessarily be deported just because you are ineligible for naturalization. On the other hand, you may be at risk of deportation even if you are eligible for naturalization. A newly added deportation provision mandates the removal of an alien convicted of a crime involving moral turpitude if the maximum possible sentence for the crime exceeds one year. Such a sentence may not be a bar to naturalization, but it is grounds for deportation. It would be prudent for you to assess your risks with proper legal advice.

CHAPTER 3

Requirements for Naturalization

The process of acquiring U.S. citizenship by an alien is called naturalization. Unlike "natural born" citizens, who have the inalienable right to citizenship by birth, aliens may acquire U.S. citizenship only on the terms and conditions established by Congress. These rules have changed over the years. Presently, to qualify for naturalization, you must:

- Be over 18 years old.
- Be a legal permanent resident.
- Have resided in the United States as a permanent resident continuously (which is different from physical presence, see below) for five years. If you are married to and living with a U.S. citizen, your continuous residency requirement is only three years.
- Have been physically present for half the continuous residency period: 30 months for most residents and 18 months for spouses of citizens.
- Have resided in the state or INS district in which the application is filed for three months.
- Be of good moral character.
- Have basic knowledge of U.S. government and history. Individuals with mental or physical disabilities may be exempt from this requirement.
- Be able to read, write and speak simple English. Some elderly, long-time permanent residents and people with disability may be exempt from this requirement.
- Express you allegiance to the United States.

Each of these requirements is discussed in detail below.

Age

To be eligible for naturalization, you must be at least 18 years old. Citizenship procedures for children are discussed in Chapter 7. Children born in the United States, even children of legal and illegal aliens, are automatically vested with U.S. citizenship. Most other children derive citizenship with the naturalization of parents.

Legal permanent residence

Citizenship is available only to individuals who are presently legal permanent residents. Some categories of war veterans are exempt from this requirement. You will be asked to produce your Alien Registration Card (I-551), more popularly known as the Green Card, to establish proof of your current legal status. If you are presently in deportation proceedings you will not be eligible for citizenship.

Continuous residence

To meet the naturalization requirements, you must have been a continuous resident of the United States for a statutory period. For most aliens this means that you must have lived continuously in the United States as a permanent resident for five years preceding your naturalization application. Spouses of U.S. citizens qualify for naturalization after only three years, provided they have been married to and are living with the same citizen spouse for the entire three year period. The spouse must also have been a citizen during the entire period.

Continuous residence does not imply that you have to be physically present in the United States. So long as the United States is your principal residence, occasional absences from the United States do not break the continuity of your residence requirement. If, however, you were absent for more than a year at a stretch, even if you had obtained a re-entry permit, it breaks the five year (or three year) residency requirement for naturalization purposes.

Under the rules, absences of less than six months do not break the continuity of residence. Absences of more than six months, but less than one year, create a presumption that continuous residency has been broken. You can overcome the presumption by establishing to the satisfaction of the INS examiner that even though you were not in the United States, you did not abandon your residence during that period and that the United States was still your primary home. Absences greater than one year break the continuity of residence, except for very narrow classes, such as employees of the

U.S. government and international treaty organizations, American businesses, etc. And even these aliens must make an application to preserve the continuity of residence (Form N-470) prior to travel.

Naturalization law also permits exceptions to the residency and physical presence requirements for spouses of U.S. citizens who are employees of the U.S. government, U.S research and religious organizations or U.S. companies engaged in foreign trade.

Physical presence

In addition to the continuous residence test, you must also meet the physical presence requirement. You must be physically present in the United States for half of the statutory period: 30 months for most permanent residents and 18 months for spouses of citizens. The physical presence test is just that: you must be physically in the United States for 30 months during the last five years (or 18 months out of the last three years for spouses). All your absences from the United States during the last five years will be added together to determine your eligibility under the physical presence test to ensure that you were physically present in the United States for at least 30 months during the last five years (18 months in the last three years if you are the spouse of a U.S. citizen).

INS district

The law also requires that you should have resided within the state or INS district in which the application is filed for at least three months. However, because you are permitted to file your application three months before meeting the statutory requirements, those who have only recently moved may file even if they have not met the three month district requirement, since the requirement will be met by the time of the examination.

A far more likely complication might arise if you move from your district before the disposition of your application, since it is currently taking upwards of two years for naturalization in many jurisdictions as a result of the backlog of applications. If you move before your application is processed, you can request the INS to transfer your application to your new district.

Continuous residence after filing

After filing your naturalization application, you must reside continuously in the United States until you have been naturalized. Absences under six months, while your application is pending, do not break the continuous residence requirement. Absences between six months to a year create a rebuttable presumption of a break in continuity and absences longer than a year break the continuity.

Good moral character

Generally, applicants must show that they are of good moral character. Good moral character is a legal term; it does not imply that you must be a paragon of virtue. You could be judged to be lacking good moral character if you have been involved in criminal activity, failed to pay child support or taxes, been convicted of drug offences or been involved in prostitution or gambling, lied in INS applications, etc. Traffic tickets, minor misdemeanors, such as disorderly conduct and the like, on the other hand, do not constitute poor moral character.

Individuals with a criminal history are best advised to discuss their record with an immigration attorney. They not only risk being denied naturalization, but they also open themselves to deportation proceedings, because many, although not all, of the grounds for the denial of naturalization for lacking good moral character are also grounds for deportation.

Not all crimes are bars to citizenship. Here is a list of some examples of crimes that are:

- A crime involving moral turpitude;
- Two or more gambling offences;
- Drug crimes, except for a single offense of simple possession of 30 grams or less of marijuana;
- Crimes for which you have been sentenced to five or more years in prison;
- A crime for which you were confined to prison for more than 180 days;
- Convictions for aggravated felony after November 1990, which increasingly includes most felonies under state and federal law.

The naturalization application asks you if you have committed a crime of moral turpitude or been involved in drug trafficking, even if you were not arrested or convicted of the crimes. You can fail the finding of good moral character if you admit to such crimes. Applicants must disclose their complete criminal record, even of crimes that are not bars to naturalization. In addition, you may fail a finding of good moral character if you:

- Are a habitual drunkard;
- Practice polygamy;
- Engaged in prostitution;
- Earned your principal income from gambling;

- Assisted in the smuggling of aliens;
- Have been involved in the trafficking of controlled substances;
- Provided false testimony for immigration benefits;
- Failed to meet your child support obligations.

If you are separated or divorced from your spouse, you may be asked to produce the divorce decree and establish that you have met your legal obligations.

The INS typically focuses on your moral character during the statutory period of the last five years — three years for spouses of citizens — but felony convictions outside the period can be considered as well. You are required to disclose criminal activity at any period in your life.

There are also several political-ideological bars to naturalization, covering anarchists, current or former communists, individuals who advocate the violent overthrow of the U.S. government, deserters, draft evaders, etc.

Language requirement

An individual must be able to read, write and speak ordinary English. The law provides that you only need have the language ability with simple words and phrases. At the interview you will be asked to read and write simple English sentences dictated by an examiner. You should be able to pass the test if you can answer oral questions at the interview. However, if questions involve detailed discussion, you have the right to conduct that part of the discussion in your native language after the examiner is satisfied that you meet the basic language requirement.

Applicants may be exempt from this requirement if they:
- have been been legal permanent residents residing in the United States for at least 15 years and are over 55 years of age;
- have been been legal permanent residents residing in the United States for at least 20 years and are over 50 years of age;
- have a medically determinable physical or mental impairment, which impairs their ability to learn English.

Knowledge of U.S. government and history

An applicant for naturalization must demonstrate a knowledge and understanding of the fundamentals of the history, principles and form of the U.S. government. Individuals with physical and mental disabilities may be exempt from the exam. Special consideration is also given to those over 65 who have been permanent residents for more than 20 years. They take a lenient test in which they are asked 10 questions from a list of 25 and are expected to answer six correctly. They are also eligible for an English language waiver and so may be tested in the language of their choice.

If you fail the language and civics test at the interview you are given a second opportunity to test for the exam within 90 days of the first interview. If you fail to appear or fail the test again, naturalization is denied.

Attachment to the constitution

Applicants must show that they are "attached to the principles of the Constitution of the United States, and well disposed to the good order and happiness of the same." They do so by taking an oath of allegiance, which requires them to swear to:

- support the U.S. Constitution and obey its laws;
- renounce any foreign allegiance and foreign title;
- bear arms for the U.S. Armed Forces or perform government service.

Applicants who can demonstrate that they are opposed to any type of military service because of religious belief are permitted to take a modified oath, which excludes the clause relating to a willingness to bear arms. The oath of allegiance is:

"I hereby declare, on oath, that I absolutely and entirely renounce and abjure all allegiance and fidelity to any foreign prince, potentate, state, or sovereignty of whom or which I have heretofore been a subject or citizen; that I will support and defend the Constitution and laws of the United States of America against all enemies, foreign and domestic; that I will bear true faith and allegiance to the same; that I will bear arms on behalf of the United States when required by the law; that I will perform noncombatant service in the Armed Forces of the United States when required by the law; that I will perform work of national importance under civilian direction when required by the law; and that I take this obligation freely without any mental reservation or purpose of evasion; so help me God."

The INS allows conscientious objectors to take the oath without the clauses: *"that I will bear arms on behalf of the United States when required by law; that I will perform noncombatant service in the Armed Forces of the United States when required by the law."*

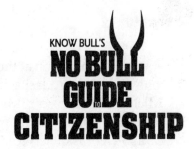

CHAPTER 4

The Naturalization Process

The naturalization process involves three very distinct steps, each of which is discussed below in detail:
• Completing the application.
• Examination by the INS.
• Oath of allegiance.

Sending for a form

Forms may be obtained from the local INS office or by calling the INS at 800-870-3676. Forms may also be requested by mail by submitting a request at the INS home page on the Internet at www.ins.usdoj.gov. Forms may also be downloaded or printed from the INS home page.

When to apply

You can file an application up to three months before meeting the continuous residence and physical residence requirements. It can currently take as long as to two years from the time you submit your application to the time you are naturalized (See Table 3), so apply as soon as you feel ready after meeting the applicable eligibility period of five years (or three years for spouses of citizens).

Where to file

The naturalization application must be filed in one of four INS Service Centers in California, Nebraska, Texas and Vermont covering the INS District in which you reside. Your application will ultimately be sent on to your INS district and your interview will also be held there. But the application needs to be filed at the service center covering your state.

File your application at the **Nebraska Service Center** if you live in the following states: Alaska, Colorado, Idaho, Illinois, Indiana, Iowa, Kansas, Michigan, Minnesota, Mississippi, Montana, Nebraska, Ohio, Oregon, South Dakota, Utah, Washington, Wisconsin and Wyoming.

USINS Nebraska Service Center
Attention N-400 Unit
P.O. Box 87400
Lincoln, NE 68501-7400
Tel: (402) 437-5218

File your application at the **Texas Service Center** if you live in the following states: Alabama, Arkansas, Florida, Georgia, Kentucky, Louisiana, Missouri, New Mexico, North Carolina, North Dakota, Oklahoma, South Carolina, Tennessee and Texas.

USINS Texas Service Center
Attention N-400 Unit
P.O. Box 851204
Mesquite, TX 75185-1204
Tel: (214) 381-1423

File your application at the **Vermont Service Center** if you live in the following states: Connecticut, Delaware, District of Columbia, Maine, Maryland, Massachusetts, New Hampshire, New Jersey, New York, Pennsylvania, Puerto Rico, Rhode Island, Vermont, Virginia and West Virginia.

USINS Vermont Service Center
Attention N-400 Unit
75 Lower Weldon Street
St Albans, VT 05479-0001
Tel: (802) 527-3160

File your application at the **California Service Center** if you live in the following states: Arizona, California, Hawaii and Nevada.

USINS California Service Center
Attention N-400 Unit
P.O. Box 10400
Laguana Nigel, CA 92607-0400
Tel: (714) 360-2769

Transfers, amendments, withdrawals

Applications may be withdrawn only with the consent of the INS district director. If the withdrawal is permitted, the application is treated as denied without prejudice to a future application. If the request for withdrawal is declined, the application will be decided on the merits.

Applicants are permitted to amend their applications to correct clerical errors stemming from omission or oversight. Substantive amendments that could affect the merits of the application are not permitted, so be careful while completing the forms. If you move while your application is pending you can request the INS to transfer your application to the district covering your new place of residence. You can submit the request up to 90 days before your move or any time after the move. You should submit your request to the INS office where your application is pending in the form of a letter, which lists your name, date of birth, alien registration number, new and old address, reason for the transfer request and the date you moved or intend to move to your new jurisdiction. INS district directors have the discretion to approve or deny transfer requests. If they consent to the transfer your application is treated as if it was originally filed in the new jurisdiction. If it is denied, your application will be adjudicated in the original INS office.

What to file

You should mail the following forms to the appropriate INS Service Center for your district:
- Completed Form N-400;
- A copy of your green card;
- Two identical photographs;
- Application fee of $225, which is effective Jan. 15, 1999 (The fee is $95 for applications filed through Jan. 15, 1999);
- An additional fingerprinting fee of $25.

A personal check is preferable for paying the fees because it will establish proof that the INS received your application if your check was cashed. You may, however, also pay by money order. It is advisable to mail your application using certified mail/return receipt requested. Be sure to photocopy your entire application. The copy will serve as a reference and you should plan on bringing the copy with you to the interview.

Photographs

You must submit two color photographs taken within 30 days of your application. Print your name and alien registration "A" number lightly on the back of each photograph in pencil. You do not need photographs of any minor children you are listing in the application form and who will be becoming citizens with you.

Most photo services are familiar with the photograph requirements. The size of the picture should be 40 mm ($1^9/_{16}$") in height by 35 mm ($1^3/_8$") in width. The photos should be glossy, untouched and unmounted with a white background. The dimension of the face should be 30 mm ($1^3/_{16}$") from the chin to top of hair and 26 mm (1") from the right ear to the left cheek. The photo should show the entire three-fourth frontal view of the right side of the face, with the right ear visible. The image should not exceed 32 mm ($1^1/_4$") in height by 28 mm ($1^1/_{16}$") in width.

Fingerprints

You must be fingerprinted by the INS and are asked to submit a $25 fee with your application to cover the fingerprinting costs. Contrary to the instructions on the Form N-400, you do not submit your fingerprints with your application. After the INS receives your application, it will send you an appointment letter with the location of the nearest INS authorized fingerprint site.

Completing the application

The first two pages of Form N-400 provide instructions on filling out the form. Type or neatly print your answers. If a question does not apply to you, write not applicable. If you are unsure of dates, indicate your best estimate and if you do not know, write "don't know." If you get help in filling out the form, be sure that you understand every question, because the INS examiner will review the application with you at your interview.

You must be thorough in completing your application. If additional space is required attach a sheet of paper with your name and alien registration number. Even minor arrests and crimes need to be identified and then explained on a separate piece of paper. An adverse answer to a question will not necessarily result in the denial of your application. Thus if you have been arrested for some minor crime, you must be sure to answer the question in the affirmative and then provide an explanation. If you are not honest in your answers and the dishonesty is caught by the INS, it will not only result in the denial of your application, it could even lead to deportation proceedings.

Part 1. Information about you

Part 1.   Information about you.

Family Name		Given Name		Middle Initial

U.S. Mailing Address - Care of

Street Number and Name			Apt. #
City		County	
State		ZIP Code	

Date of Birth (month/day/year)	Country of Birth
Social Security #	A #

In the section, you are required to provide your name, address, date and country of birth and social security and alien registration number. List the name you want to appear on your naturalization certificate. All communications from the INS will be sent to you at this address. The naturalization process allows you an opportunity to legally change your name and if you wish to make changes to your name, you can so request at the interview.

Part 2. Basis for eligibility

Part 2.   Basis for Eligibility *(check one).*

a. ☐ I have been a permanent resident for at least five (5) years .

b. ☐ I have been a permanent resident for at least three (3) years and have been married to a United States Citizen for those three years.

c. ☐ I am a permanent resident child of United States citizen parent(s) .

d. ☐ I am applying on the basis of qualifying military service in the Armed Forces of the U.S. and have attached completed Forms N-426 and G-325B

e. ☐ Other. (Please specify section of law)_____.

Check (a) if you have been a permanent resident for five or more years.

Check (b) if you have been and currently are married to and living with a U.S. citizen spouse for three or more years.

Option (c) is no longer valid. You no longer file naturalization applications for children; apply instead for a certificate of citizenship.

Check (d) if you are a military veteran.

Check (e) if you are an applicant in a special class, such as widows of servicemen, spouses of U.S. citizens stationed abroad, employees of U.S. news media organizations, former U.S. citizens, etc.

Part 3. Additional information about you

Part 3. Additional information about you.

Date you became a permanent resident (month/day/year)	Port admitted with an immmigrant visa or INS Office where granted adjustment of status.

Citizenship

Name on alien registration card (if different than in Part 1)

Other names used since you became a permanent resident (including maiden name)

Sex ☐ Male ☐ Female	Height	Marital Status: ☐ Single ☐ Married	☐ Divorced ☐ Widowed

Can you speak, read and write English ?   ☐No ☐Yes.

Absences from the U.S.:

Have you been absent from the U.S. since becoming a permanent resident?   ☐ No ☐Yes.

If you answered **"Yes"** , complete the following, Begin with your most recent absence. If you need more room to explain the reason for an absence or to list more trips, continue on separate paper.

Date left U.S.	Date returned	Did absence last 6 months or more?		Destination	Reason for trip
		Yes	No		
		Yes	No		
		Yes	No		
		Yes	No		
		Yes	No		
		Yes	No		

In this section you are asked to list the date you became a permanent resident and the port you were admitted or the INS office where you adjusted your status. This information is on the back of your alien card. This section also asks you about your current citizenship, whether the name on your alien card is different than the one you are now indicating in Part 1 and any other names you may have used since becoming a permanent resident. If you have changed your name, for instance, through marriage or use aliases, and many aliens adopt Christian aliases, you should indicate that here. The form also asks for your sex, height and marital status. You are also asked if you can speak, read and write English. Unless you are exempt from the language requirement, this is an eligibility standard.

The most important section in this part, however, inquires about your absences from the United States. This information is used to determine your continuous residency and physical presence requirements.

You are asked to list all absences from the United States since you became a permanent resident, including the date you left the United States and the date you returned. You are also asked to specify if any absence lasted more than six months. An absence briefer than six months does not break your continuous residence requirement, but any individual absence longer than six months creates a presumption that you have broken continuity of residence. You can rebut that presumption by demonstrating that the United States was still your primary home, notwithstanding the lengthy absence. Expect to be quizzed if you have frequent and extended absences (lasting 6 months but less than a year) from the United States. If you were outside the United States for more than one year during the last five years (three years if you are married to a U.S. citizen) you have broken your continuous residence and will not be able to meet that requirement.

In addition, you must have been physically present in the United States for 30 months during the last five years (18 months of the last three years if you are married to a U.S. citizen). Carefully calculate that you have in fact met the physical requirement test by adding up all the days you were physically present in the United States. There are some rare exceptions to the requirement for people serving in the military and U.S. government employees.

Part 4. Information about residences and employment

In this section you are asked to list all your addresses during the last five years or since you became permanent resident, whichever is less. You must also list your employment history during the past five years. You can't be denied naturalization because you were not employed or received public benefits. So do not hesitate to answer this question truthfully.

You will be asked to produce your tax returns by the INS and failure to file tax returns can result in the denial of your application. Unless you earned

Part 4. Information about your residences and employment.

A. List your addresses during the last five (5) years or since you became a permanent resident, whichever is less. Begin with your current address. If you need more space, continue on separate paper:

Street Number and Name, City, State, Country, and Zip Code	Dates (month/day/year)	
	From	To

B. List your employers during the last five (5) years. List your present or most recent employer first. If none, write "None". If you need more space, continue on separate paper.

Employer's Name	Employer's Address	Dates Employed (month/day/year)		Occupation/position
	Street Name and Number - City, State and ZIP Code	From	To	

so little income that you are exempt from filing tax returns, it is critical that you meet IRS tax obligations.

Another area of concern in this section is if you secured permanent residence through sponsorship by an employer. The fact that you left your sponsoring employer does not preclude your naturalization and the law does not require that you be employed by your sponsor for any specific length of time. However, you should be prepared to be questioned by the examiner about the reasons you switched employment.

Part 5. Information about your marital history

Part 5. Information about your marital history.

A. Total number of times you have been married ____ . If you are now married, complete the following regarding your husband or wife.

Family name	Given name	Middle initial
Address		
Date of birth (month/day/year)	Country of birth	Citizenship
Social Security#	A# (if applicable)	Immigration status (If not a U.S. citizen)
Naturalization (If applicable) (month/day/year)	Place (City, State)	

If you have ever previously been married or if your current spouse has been previously married, please provide the following on separate paper: Name of prior spouse, date of marriage, date marriage ended, how marriage ended and immigration status of prior spouse.

In this section you are asked to detail your marital history. For those who are qualifying for naturalization under the shorter three year continuous residence requirement to which spouses of U.S. citizens are eligible, this information must demonstrate that you have been married to and lived with the citizen spouse for the full three year period.

If you secured permanent residence through a spouse and are now separated or divorced, expect to be questioned about the marriage because the INS investigates fraudulent marriages for securing green cards. The information you provide here, in case of separation or divorce, will also be relevant in determining whether you have met your child support obligations, which are factors in a finding of good moral character.

Part 6. Information about your children

Part 6. Information about your children.

B. Total Number of Children _____ . Complete the following information for each of your children. If the child lives with you, state "with me" in the address column; otherwise give city/state/country of child's current residence. If deceased, write "deceased" in the address column. If you need more space, continue on separate paper.

Full name of child	Date of birth	Country of birth	Citizenship	A - Number	Address

Here you must list the names, date of birth, addresses and citizenship status of all your children. If non adult children are not living with you and you are separated or divorced, expect to be scrutinized about your child support obligations.

This information is also relevant for determining derivative citizenship for children. Children under 18 years of age, who are permanent residents, will automatically acquire U.S. citizenship at your naturalization, regardless of whether they meet the continuous residence and physical presence requirements. They are not required to take the language and civics test, nor the oath of allegiance.

Children under 18 will automatically be naturalized if they meet the following requirements:
- The child's other parent is a citizen.
- Both of the child's parents are being naturalized at the same time.
- The naturalizing parent is divorced or separated and has legal custody of the child.
- The child's other parent is deceased.
- The child's mother is naturalizing and the child was born out of wedlock.

- The child's father is naturalizing and the child was born out of wed-lock, but had been legitimated by the father.

Part 7. Additional eligibility factors

Part 7. Additional eligibility factors.

Please answer each of the following questions. If your answer is **"Yes"**, explain on a separate paper.

1.	Are you now, or have you ever been a member of, or in any way connected or associated with the Communist Party, or ever knowingly aided or supported the Communist Party directly, or indirectly through another organization, group or person, or ever advocated, taught, believed in, or knowingly supported or furthered the interests of communism?	Yes	No
2.	During the period March 23, 1933 to May 8, 1945, did you serve in, or were you in any way affiliated with, either directly or indirectly, any military unit, paramilitary unit, police unit, self-defense unit, vigilante unit, citizen unit of the Nazi party or SS, government agency or office, extermination camp, concentration camp, prisoner of war camp, prison, labor camp, detention camp or transit camp, under the control or affiliated with:		
	a. The Nazi Government of Germany?	Yes	No
	b. Any government in any area occupied by, allied with, or established with the assistance or cooperation of, the Nazi Government of Germany?	Yes	No
3.	Have you at any time, anywhere, ever ordered, incited, assisted, or otherwise participated in the persecution of any person because of race, religion, national origin, or political opinion?	Yes	No
4.	Have you ever left the United States to avoid being drafted into the U.S. Armed Forces?	Yes	No
5.	Have you ever failed to comply with Selective Service laws?	Yes	No
	If you have registered under the Selective Service laws, complete the following information:		
	Selective Service Number:_____ Date Registered:_____		
	If you registered before 1978, also provide the following:		
	Local Board Number:_____ Classification:_____		
6.	Did you ever apply for exemption from military service because of alienage, conscientious objections or other reasons?	Yes	No
7.	Have you ever deserted from the military, air or naval forces of the United States?	Yes	No
8.	Since becoming a permanent resident , have you ever failed to file a federal income tax return ?	Yes	No
9.	Since becoming a permanent resident , have you filed a federal income tax return as a nonresident or failed to file a federal return because you considered yourself to be a nonresident?	Yes	No
10	Are deportation proceedings pending against you, or have you ever been deported, or ordered deported, or have you ever applied for suspension of deportation?	Yes	No
11.	Have you ever claimed in writing, or in any way, to be a United States citizen?	Yes	No
12.	Have you ever:		
	a. been a habitual drunkard?	Yes	No
	b. advocated or practiced polygamy?	Yes	No
	c. been a prostitute or procured anyone for prostitution?	Yes	No
	d. knowingly and for gain helped any alien to enter the U.S. illegally?	Yes	No
	e. been an illicit trafficker in narcotic drugs or marijuana?	Yes	No
	f. received income from illegal gambling?	Yes	No
	g. given false testimony for the purpose of obtaining any immigration benefit?	Yes	No
13.	Have you ever been declared legally incompetent or have you ever been confined as a patient in a mental institution?	Yes	No
14.	Were you born with, or have you acquired in same way, any title or order of nobility in any foreign State?	Yes	No
15.	Have you ever:		
	a. knowingly committed any crime for which you have not been arrested?	Yes	No
	b. been arrested, cited, charged, indicted, convicted, fined or imprisoned for breaking or violating any law or ordinance excluding traffic regulations?	Yes	No

(If you answer yes to 15 , in your explanation give the following information for each incident or occurrence the **city**, **state**, and **country**, where the offense took place, the **date** and **nature** of the offense, and the **outcome** or **disposition** of the case).

In this section you are asked to respond to 15 questions, which are de-signed to establish your good moral character and affinity for the United States. If you answer "yes" to any question, you run the risk of not only being denied naturalization, but also of being deported, because many, though not all, of the grounds for denial of naturalization under these eligi-bility factors, are also grounds for deportation. You must answer this sec-tion truthfully and fully, because your application can also be denied if you knowingly provide false information and falsifying information also places you at risk of deportation. In addition, lying in your naturalization application is among the very few grounds for denaturalization, because the naturalization is considered to have been illegally acquired. If you have any doubts about your response to any of these questions you are advised to discuss your situation with a qualified immigration attorney.

Question 1. Communists

Current members of communist organizations are prohibited from naturalization. Former members may be naturalized if at least 10 years have lapsed since they left the organization. The INS permits certain exceptions if your communist membership was involuntary or coerced for economic or other reasons. Naturalization may be permitted of former communist members if their membership terminated before they turned 16.

Question 2. Nazis

World War II Nazis are permanently barred from naturalization.

Question 3. Persecutors

If you participated in the persecution of any person because of their race, religion, national origin or political opinion, you are barred from becoming a U.S. citizen.

Question 4. Draft evaders

If you left the country to escape the draft you are prohibited from naturalization. There is an exception for men who left the country between Aug 4, 1964, and March 28, 1973, who were all pardoned by Pres. Jimmy Carter.

Question 5. Selective service obligations

Young men between the ages of 18 and 25 born after Jan 1, 1960, are required to register with the selective service. The rule applies to citizens, permanent residents and illegal aliens. Non-immigrants are exempt from the requirement. If you are a male born after Jan 1, 1960, were a permanent resident in the United States between the age of 18 to 25 and failed to register with selective service you can face a problem with your naturalization application. If you were unaware of your obligation to register and didn't get a notice to register from the INS or the selective service, you can execute an affidavit to the INS examiner at your interview that your failure to register was not knowing and willful and you may still be naturalized.

If you "knowingly and willfully" failed to register, however, you must wait at least five years after your registration obligation ended, i.e. until you are 31, before you can be naturalized. Spouses of U.S. citizens can be naturalized three years after their registration obligations ended, i.e. when they turn 29.

For additional information regarding selective service, or if you need to get your registration number if you had registered, call 847-688-6888.

Question 6. Exemption from the draft

If you applied for exemption from military service after you were drafted because of your alienage you are barred from naturalization. You may be able to argue a defense that you were not obligated to serve if your draft number didn't come up, or that your request for waiver was unknowing or that you didn't understand your obligations. If you sought or received exemption on conscientious objector grounds you are not barred from citizenship.

Question 7. Wartime deserters

Wartime deserters are barred from U.S. citizenship, with the exception of Vietnam War deserters, who received a presidential pardon from Pres. Carter.

Question 8. Federal tax returns

You can be denied naturalization if you failed to file income tax returns since you became a permanent resident, unless you can demonstrate that you were not required to file such returns because your income fell below the income tax threshold. The INS examiner may ask to see your IRS returns for the last five years.

Question 9. Non resident tax return

If you claimed nonresident status for tax purposes, you may be considered to have abandoned your U.S. residence and be ineligible for naturalization.

Question 10. Deportation proceedings

Your naturalization application will not be processed if you are presently in any stage of a deportation proceeding. If you have been involved in deportation proceedings in the past, the INS will want to scrutinize the reasons behind those proceedings, which could potentially adversely affect your application. If you are presently a legal permanent resident and the deportation proceedings involved an earlier period of your stay in the United States, however, it should not preclude your naturalization.

Question 11. Claim to U.S. citizenship

You should not have made any false claims to U.S. citizenship.

Question 12. Immoral acts

If you have been a habitual drunkard, practiced polygamy, trafficked in drugs, smuggled aliens, been involved in prostitution or illegal gambling, or given false information to the INS, you are at risk of being denied naturalization. If the acts took place before the statutory period of five years (three if you are married to a U.S. citizen) you may be able to overcome the ineligibility by establishing your good moral character since.

Question 13. Mental competence

Mental disability is not itself a bar to naturalization unless you are legally incompetent and lack the mental capability to understand the oath of allegiance.

Question 14. Title or nobility

You are asked to disclose any formal titles or order of nobility. If you possess any titles, you will be asked to renounce them at the swearing in ceremony.

Question 15. Criminal acts

Here you are asked to list any criminal activity you might have engaged in, even if you were not charged or convicted for it. Some serious crimes are permanent bars to naturalization. If the acts occurred before your statutory period, the INS may still permit you to be naturalized. But you are advised to discuss your situation with an immigration attorney. A person convicted of a crime of moral turpitude, drug related crimes and those confined for more than 180 days in prison are permanently barred from naturalization. People convicted of aggravated felonies at any time are likewise permanently barred from citizenship.

Part 8. Allegiance to the United States

Part 8. Allegiance to the U.S.		
If your answer to any of the following questions is "NO", attach a full explanation:		
1. Do you believe in the Constitution and form of government of the U.S.?	Yes	No
2. Are you willing to take the full Oath of Allegiance to the U.S.? (see instructions)	Yes	No
3. If the law requires it, are you willing to bear arms on behalf of the U.S.?	Yes	Ho
4. If the law requires it, are you willing to perform noncombatant services in the Armed Forces of the U.S.?	Yes	No
5. If the law requires it, are you willing to perform work of national importance under civilian direction?	Yes	No

You must establish your fidelity to the U.S. form of government by answering in the affirmative to this question. The law permits no exception to this requirement. You must also express a willingness to take the oath of allegiance and be willing to bear arms and perform noncombatant or civil service. Conscientious objectors may for religious reasons omit the section of the oath on performing armed service, but the exception is available only on religious grounds, not because of political, social, philosophical views or a personal moral code. You must still be willing to perform civilian service.

Part 9. Memberships and organizations

Part 9. Memberships and organizations.
A.   List your present and past membership in or affiliation with every organization, association, fund, foundation, party, club, society, or similar group in the United States or in any other place. Include any military service in this part. If none, write "none". Include the name of organization, location, dates of membership and the nature of the organization. If additional space is needed, use separate paper.

You are asked to list all organizations to which you belong. The principal function of this question is to determine whether you might fall under excludable classes through memberships in communist and other excludable organizations.

Part 10. Children

Part 10. Complete only if you checked block " C " in Part 2.

How many of your parents are U.S. citizens?   One   Both   (Give the following about one U.S. citizen parent:)

Family Name	Given Name	Middle Name

Address

Basis for citizenship:
  Birth
  Naturalization Cert. No. | Relationship to you (check one):   natural parent   adoptive parent
  parent of child legitimated after birth

If adopted or legitimated after birth, give date of adoption or, legitimation: *(month/day/year)_____.*

Does this parent have legal custody of you?   Yes   No

(Attach a copy of relating evidence to establish that you are the child of this U.S. citizen and evidence of this parent's citizenship.)

This section is no longer valid, because children no longer apply for naturalization.

Part 11. Signature

Part 11. Signature.   *(Read the information on penalties in the instructions before completing this section).*

I certify or, if outside the United States, I swear or affirm, under penalty of perjury under the laws of the United States of America that this application, and the evidence submitted with it, is all true and correct. I authorize the release of any information from my records which the Immigration and Naturalization Service needs to determine eligibility for the benefit I am seeking.

Signature   **Date**

Please Note: *If you do not completely fill out this form, or fail to submit required documents listed in the instructions, you may not be found eligible for naturalization and this application may be denied.*

Part 12. Signature of person preparing form if other than above. *(Sign below)*

I declare that I prepared this application at the request of the above person and it is based on all information of which I have knowledge.
Signature   Print Your Name   Date

Firm Name
and Address

DO NOT COMPLETE THE FOLLOWING UNTIL INSTRUCTED TO DO SO AT THE INTERVIEW

I swear that I know the contents of this application, and supplemental pages 1 through____, that the corrections , numbered 1 through____, were made at my request, and that this amended application, is true to the best of my knowledge and belief.

Subscribed and sworn to before me by the applicant.

(Examiner's Signature)   Date

(Complete and true signature of applicant)

You must sign and date your application. If someone assisted in preparing the form you, they must also sign the form in Part 12.

Do not sign the section at the bottom of the form that reads "Do not complete the following until instructed to do so at the interview." This section will be signed by you under oath at the time of the INS interview before an examiner.

CHAPTER 5

The Citizenship Test

As part of the naturalization process you are required to take an oral civics test. INS examiners are instructed to ask questions based on an applicant's age, background and period of residency in the United States from a standardized list of 100 questions. Examiners have discretion in determining which and how many questions to ask and some are known to have asked as few as one or two. Typically, most examiners ask from six to 10 questions and expect you to answer half correctly to pass.

For a period, the INS permitted outside centers to conduct these exams and such tests taken before Aug 30, 1998, when the program was terminated, can be used through Aug 30, 1999. Presently, this examination is taken at the interview. The INS has tested a pilot program at four centers, which could result in the exam being held prior to an interview at INS Application Support Centers during the fingerprinting process. If and when such a program is implemented, applicants may be able to take a written multiple choice test in which they will be expected to answer 12 of 20 questions correctly.

The physically and mentally impaired can be exempt from the exam. The INS also gives special consideration to those over 65 who have been permanent residents for more than 20 years. They are administered a lenient test in which they are asked 10 questions from a list of 25 and are expected to answer six correctly. They are also eligible for an English language waiver and so may be tested in the language of their choice.

If you fail the language and civics test at the interview, you are given another opportunity to test for the exam within 90 days of the first interview. If you fail to appear or fail the test again, naturalization is denied.

The list of questions and answers used by INS examiners for the civics test follow. You can practice the test by covering up the answers provided in the right column on the next several pages.

The Citizenship Test

Questions	Answers
1. What are the colors of our flag?	1. Red, white and blue.
2. How many stars are there in our flag?	2. 50.
3. What color are the stars on our flag?	3. White.
4. What do the stars on the flag mean?	4. One for each state in the Union.
5. How many stripes are there in the flag?	5. 13.
6. What color are the stripes?	6. Red and white.
7. What do the stripes on the flag mean?	7. They represent the 13 original states.
8. How many states are there in the union?	8. 50.
9. What is the 4th of July?	9. Independence Day.
10. What is the date of Independence Day?	10. July 4th.
11. Independence from whom?	11. England.
12. What country did we fight in the Revolutionary War?	12. England.
13. Who was the first President of the United States?	13. George Washington.

Questions	Answers
14. Who is the President of United States today?	14. William "Bill" Jefferson Clinton.
15. Who is the Vice President of the United States today?	15. Al Gore.
16. Who elects the President of the United States?	16. The Electoral College.
17. Who becomes President of the United States if the President should die?	17. Vice President.
18. For how long do we elect the President?	18. Four years.
19. What is the Constitution?	19. The supreme law of the land.
20. Can the Constitution be changed?	20. Yes.
21. What do we call a change to the Constitution?	21. Amendments.
22. How many changes or amendments are there to the Constitution?	22.. 27 (with the Congressional Pay amendment ratified May 7, 1992).
23. How many branches are there in our government?	23. Three.
24. What are the three branches of our government?	24. Legislative, executive and judiciary.
25. What is the legislative branch of our government?	25. Congress.

Questions

26. *You go* Who makes the laws in the United States?

27. What is Congress?

28. What are the duties of Congress?

29. Who elects Congress?

30. How many senators are there in Congress?

31. Can you name the two senators from your state?

32. For how long do we elect each senator?

33. How many representatives are there in Congress?

34. For how long do we elect the representatives?

35. What is the executive branch of our government?

36. What is the judiciary branch of our government?

37. What are the duties of the Supreme Court?

38. What is the supreme law of the United States?

Answers

26. Congress.

27. The Senate and the House of Representatives.

28. To make laws.

29. The people.

30. 100.

31. Varies by state. Check your local library.

32. Six years.

33. 435.

34. Two years.

35. The president, Cabinet and departments under the Cabinet members.

36. The Supreme Court.

37. To interpret laws.

38. The Constitution.

Questions	Answers
39. What is the Bill of Rights?	39. The first 10 amendments to the Constitution.
40. What is the capital of your state?	40. Varies by state. Check your local library.
41. Who is the current governor of your state?	41. Varies by state. Check your local library.
42. Who becomes President of the U.S.A. if the President and Vice President should die?	42. Speaker of the House of Representatives.
43. Who is the Chief Justice of the Supreme Court?	43. William Rehnquist.
44. Can you name the thirteen original states?	44. Connecticut, New Hampshire, New York, New Jersey, Massachusetts, Pennsylvania, Delaware, Virginia, North Carolina, South Carolina, Georgia, Rhode Island & Maryland.
45. Who said: "Give me liberty or give me death"?	45. Patrick Henry.
46. Which countries were our enemies during World War II?	46. Germany, Italy and Japan.
47. What are the 49th and 50th States of the Union?	47. Alaska and Hawaii.
48. How many terms can a President serve?	48. Two.

Questions	Answers
49. Who was Martin Luther King, Jr. ?	49. A civil rights leader.
50. Who is the head of your local government?	50. The mayor of your city or top executive of your county, depending on where you live. Check your local library.
51. According to the Constitution, a person must meet certain requirements in order to be eligible to become President. Name one of these requirements.	51. Must be a natural born citizen of the United States; must be at least 35 years old by the time he or she will serve; must have lived in the United States for at least 14 years.
52. Why are there 100 senators in the Senate?	52. Two from each state.
53. Who selects the Supreme Court Justices?	53. Appointed by the President.
54. How many Supreme Court Justices are there?	54. Nine.
55. Why did the pilgrims come to America?	55. For religious freedom.
56. What is the head executive of a state government called?	56. Governor.
57. What is the head executive of a city government called?	57. Mayor.
58. What holiday was celebrated for the first time by the American Colonists?	58. Thanksgiving.

Questions	Answers
59. Who was the main writer of the Declaration of Independence?	59. Thomas Jefferson.
60. When was the Declaration of Independence adopted?	60. July 4, 1776.
61. What is the basic belief of the Declaration of Independence?	61. That all men are created equal.
62. What is the National Anthem of the United States?	62. The Star-Spangled Banner.
63. Who wrote The Star Spangled Banner?	63. Francis Scott Key.
64. Where does Freedom of Speech come from?	64. The Bill of Rights.
65. What is the minimum voting age in the United States?	65. Eighteen.
66. Who signs bills into law?	66. The President.
67. What is the highest court in the United States?	67. The Supreme Court.
68. Who was President during the Civil War?	68. Abraham Lincoln.
69. What did the Emancipation Proclamation do?	69. Freed many slaves.
70. What special group advises the President?	70. The Cabinet.

NO BULL GUIDE TO CITIZENSHIP ■

Questions

71. Which President is called the Father of Our Country?

72. What Immigration and Naturalization Service form is used to apply for naturalized citizenship?

73. Who helped the Pilgrims in America?

74. The first Pilgrims sailed to America in what ship?

75. What were the 13 original states of the United States called?

76. Name three rights or freedoms guaranteed by the Bill of Rights.

77. Who has the power to declare war?

78. What kind of government does the United States have?

79. Which President freed the slaves?

Answers

71. George Washington.

72. Form N-400, Application to File Petition for Naturalization.

73. The American Indians (Native Americans).

74. The Mayflower.

75. Colonies.

76. Freedom of speech, press, religion, and assembly. The right to bear arms. The right to a jury trial. The right against warrantless searches, self incrimination, trial twice for the same crime, and excessive fines and unusual and cruel punishment.

77. The Congress.

78. Republican.

79. Abraham Lincoln.

Questions	Answers
80. In what year was the Constitution written?	80. 1787.
81. What are the first 10 Amendments to the Constitution called?	81. The Bill of Rights.
82. Name one purpose of the United Nations.	82. For countries to discuss world problems; to provide economic aid to many countries.
83. Where does Congress meet?	83. In the Capitol, in Washington, D.C.
84. Whose rights are guaranteed by the Constitution and the Bill of Rights?	84. Everyone (citizens and non-citizens living in the U.S.).
85. What is the introduction to the Constitution called?	85. The Preamble.
86. Name one benefit of being a citizen of the United States.	86. Obtain federal jobs; travel with a U.S. passport; petition for close relatives to come to the United States to live.
87. What is the most important right granted to U.S. citizens?	87. The right to vote.
88. What is the United States Capitol?	88. The place where Congress meets.
89. What is the White House?	89. The president's official residence.
90. Where is the White House located?	90. Washington, D.C.; 1600 Pennsylvania Ave., NW.

Questions

91. What is the name of the President's official home?

92. Name one right guaranteed by the First Amendment.

93. Who is the Commander-in-Chief of the U.S. military?

94. Which President was the first Commander-in-Chief of the U.S. military?

95. In what month do we vote for the President?

96. In what month is the new President inaugurated?

97. How many times may a senator be re-elected?

98. How many times may a congressman be re-elected?

99. What are the 2 major political parties in the U.S. today?

100. How many states are there in the United States?

Answers

91. The White House.

92. Freedom of speech, press, religion, peaceable assembly and petitioning for changes in government.

93. The President.

94. George Washington.

95. November.

96. January.

97. There is no limit.

98. There is no limit.

99. Democratic and Republican.

100. Fifty.

65/20 Citizenship Test

Applicants over 65 who have been permanent residents for more than 20 years take a simpler test from the following list of 25 questions. You must be able to answer six out of ten questions selected by an INS examiner.

Questions

1. Why do we celebrate the Fourth of July?

2. Who was the first President of the United States?

3. Who is the President of the United States?

4. What is the Constitution?

5. What are the first ten amendments to the Constitution called?

6. Who elects Congress?

7. How many senators are there in Congress?

8. For how long do we elect each Senator?

9. For how long do we elect the representatives in Congress?

10. Who nominates judges to the Supreme Court?

11. What are the three branches of our government?

Answers

1. Independence Day.

2. George Washington.

3. William Jefferson Clinton.

4. The supreme law of the land.

5. The Bill of Rights.

6. The people.

7. 100.

8. Six years

9. Two years.

10. The President.

11. Legislative, Executive and Judiciary.

Questions

12. What is the highest court in the United States?

13. What major river running north to south divides the United States?

14. The Civil War was fought over what important issue?

15. Name the two major political parties in the United States?

16. How many states are in the United States?

17. What is the capital of the United States?

18. What is the minimum voting age in the United States?

19. Who was Martin Luther King, Jr.?

20. What nation was the first to land a man on the moon?

21. What is the capital of your state?

22. What is it called if the president refuses to sign a bill?

23. What two oceans bound the United States?

Answers

12. U.S. Supreme Court.

13. The Mississippi River.

14. Slavery and States Rights.

15. Democratic and Republican.

16. Fifty.

17. Washington, D.C.

18. Eighteen.

19. A civil rights leader.

20. United States of America.

21. Varies. Check with your local library.

22. Veto.

23. The Atlantic and Pacific Oceans.

Questions	Answers
24. What famous American invented the electric light bulb?	24. Thomas Edison.
25. What is the national anthem of the United States?	25. The Star-Spangled Banner.

Testing yourself on the INS Home Page

The INS has set up a self-test on its web site where you can practice and test your knowledge of U.S. history and civics. You can generate questions and will be evaluated on your practice answers by going to: http://www.insdoj.gov/exec/natz/natztest.asp

Welcome to the *Naturalization* Self-Test

Welcome to the Naturalization Self Test! To begin the self test, click the **Generate Questions** button.

This is a test of your knowledge of United States History and the structure of our government. This is not the actual test that you will be given by an INS Officer. It is designed to be used as a study guide only. The study guide test is in multiple choice format. At your interview, the INS Officer will ask you similar questions in an oral format. You will also be evaluated on your ability to speak, read, write, and understand English at your interview.

CHAPTER 6

After the Filing

After the application is received by the INS Service Center it is reviewed. It may be returned to you if it is incomplete, if you have failed to provide some information or the attached material, such as fees or photographs. The agency may also occasionally request additional information. The data in the application is entered and your permanent file is requested from all 80 INS locations. A temporary file is created if the file is not found after a 90-day search.

Fingerprinting
Between two weeks to 90 days after the filing you will receive an appointment letter asking you to appear at the closest of one of 127 INS Application Service Centers (ASC) for fingerprinting. You are asked to appear at the centers during a given week. The centers are located in major metros throughout the country and many have evening and weekend hours. You must appear at the fingerprint facility with a valid identification, such as an alien card or a photo ID. If you are unable to keep your appointment during the assigned week you can appear for fingerprinting on a first-come first-serve basis on any Wednesday within 84 days of the originally scheduled appointment or your application will be considered abandoned.

The fingerprint cards are sent on to the Service Center, where the fingerprints are transferred onto a machine readable data tape and both the card and the tape are forwarded to the FBI, which checks the fingerprints against criminal databases and responds back to the Service Center. The average time for an FBI response varies from 30 to 45 days. The naturalization interview will be scheduled only after the fingerprint clearance has been received from the FBI.

The Interview Notification

Applications are reviewed and adjudicated at the INS District Office, where your file is forwarded after the FBI background check. The local office assigns the case to an examiner and your interview is scheduled.

During the past several decades, the number of naturalization applications ranged from 100,000 to 300,000. The past few years have experienced a surge in applications, driven partly by the political concerns over restrictions on immigration and welfare reforms that deny benefits to noncitizens. In 1997, the INS received 1.6 million applications, nearly five times the number it received at the start of the decade. Consequently, there is a backlog of nearly 2 million applications, resulting in significant delays between the time you file your application and are scheduled for an interview, which varies from under six months in Pittsburgh, Pa., and Hartford, Conn., to well over two years in Atlanta, Ga., and Tampa, Fla., (Table 2).

The INS claims that it expects to reduce the delay to under a year by the end of 1999, and the recent decline in new citizenship applications should relieve some of the delays. The interviews may be expedited in the case of spouses of citizens who are taking up overseas employment and because of health problems of a serious nature.

At some point, which varies from six months to two years, depending upon your INS district, you will receive a notification from the INS giving you the time and place to appear for the preliminary examination. Your eligibility for naturalization is determined at the interview.

Interview

During the interview, the INS examiner will explain the nature of the interview and that it is being conducted under oath. He will review your application to determine that you meet the residency and physical presence requirements, are of good moral character, have knowledge of U.S. history and government, and possess the ability to read write and speak English. If you are exempt from any of the requirements, the INS examiner will not go through these tests.

The naturalization application includes much of the information the INS examiner needs to determine whether the applicant meets the naturalization requirements. Most of the interview will center round a review of your application. The officer will examine the application with you and make any changes to it based on your oral testimony. Your answers to the examiner's questions will assess your competence in the English language.

Table 3
Naturalization Application Processing Time

District	Filing Until Interview	Swearing In After Interview
Albuquerque	565-745	14-21
Atlanta	730-1095	330-365
Baltimore	240	1
Boston	300	90
Buffalo	360-390	60-90
Charlotte	730-790	30-90
Chicago	540-720	30-90
Cincinnati	300-360	120-180
Cleveland	300-360	120-180
Dallas	450-520	140-180
Denver	365-515	1
Detroit	270-365	15-30
El Paso	480-570	30
Harlingen	450	90-120
Hartford	150	30
Honolulu	150-180	20-30
Houston	480-520	60-90
Indianapolis	180-210	15-45
Kansas City	180-240	20-50
Las Vegas	240	90
Louisville	365-540	30
Los Angeles	365-485	30-60
Memphis	240-270	90-120
Miami	360-390	90-120
Milwaukee	545-570	60-180

Disrict	Filing Until Interview	Swearing In After Interview
New Orleans	270-550	30-360
New York	360-510	45
Newark	365-425	1
Oklahoma City	365-540	90-120
Omaha	300-365	30-40
Orlando	240	120
Philadelphia	270-360	30-60
Phoenix	540-630	210
Pittsburgh	60-90	10-40
Portland	720	60-90
Sacramento	515	30-90
San Antonio	350-390	90-150
San Francisco	390-480	30-120
San Jose	240-730	30-640
Seattle	240-300	1
St. Paul	180-240	90-120
Salt Lake City	270-300	60-90
Tampa	720-900	14-64
Washington DC/VA	300	14

Source: American Immigration Lawyers Association. Number in column 2 represents the number of days between filing of application and the INS interview. Number in column 3 is the number of days between the INS interview and the swearing-in ceremony. Estimate as of June 1998.

The examiner also administers a short dictation. He will also ask you some questions on U.S. history. These tests are not intended to trick or trip you up. Typically the examiner asks about a dozen questions, sometimes even fewer, and will accept some wrong answers.

If you fail to meet any of the requirements, for instance, if you fail the language or civics test, the examiner may suggest that you retake the exam, while filing the petition anyway. If there are other deficiencies in the application, the examiner may continue the examination to a later date to allow you time to overcome the deficiencies. Applicants who have problems may submit additional evidence and another interview is scheduled. The examiner will inform you of the deficiencies in writing and ask they be addressed at the second interview. Failure to appear at the second interview or to provide additional documentation will result in the INS adjudicating the application on the merits with the information on the record. If you are unable to overcome the deficiencies the application may be denied.

Often the examiner will decide on your application at the interview. But sometimes the determination can be withheld. The law requires that the INS must make a decision to grant or deny within 120 days of the interview. If the INS has not made a decision on your application within that time, you have the right to seek a review by the federal district court in your jurisdiction.

Toward the end of the interview you will be asked to subscribe under oath the application as well as a formal Petition for Naturalization, Form N-405. Children who automatically become citizens through their parent's naturalization should come to the examination, but are not required to pass the English or citizenship test. Children under 14 do not have to take the oath of allegiance either.

If your citizenship application is denied because you fail the language or civic test, you are permitted another chance to pass the test. The application is denied if you fail to reappear for the tests or fail them again. You can also reapply for citizenship and there are no limits on how often you can reapply.

A supervisor reviews all denials as well as all approvals of applicants with criminal records, if the permanent file is missing, or if the applicant has applied for a disability waiver. If an application is denied you can seek an administrative review before an immigration officer within 30 days of the denial. If the denial is not reversed at the administrative hearing, you can seek a review in federal district court within 120 days.

If an application is approved, the database is updated, a naturalization certificate is printed and you are notified to appear at an oath ceremony, which depending upon jurisdiction, may be at a court or at an INS office.

Naturalization ceremony

The last and final step in the naturalization process is the swearing in ceremony. You will be scheduled for a citizenship oath ceremony once your application is approved. Usually you have the option of being sworn in at an INS ceremony or one at a court. The oath ceremony is also an opportunity to change your name as part of the naturalization process and those planning on doing so must opt for a court ceremony because only courts are authorized to change names and the name change becomes affective at the oath ceremony. INS ceremonies are typically faster.

You will receive notification on Form N-445A to participate in a ceremony at which you take the pledge of allegiance. The timing of the ceremony depends upon your place of residence, as these ceremonies may take place weekly in some areas and every few months in others. Usually, you will be called for the ceremony within two weeks to three months (see Table 3) after the interview, although delays of up to a year are reported in San Jose, Calif., Atlanta, Ga., and Louisville, Ky. Children under the age of 14 need not attend the ceremony.

At the ceremony you take the oath of allegiance. The judge signs the order for naturalization and you receive a Certificate of Naturalization (Form N-550) which documents your new citizenship. You will be asked to surrender your alien registration card (green card) at this time. In some jurisdictions, if the naturalization ceremony is very large, the certificate may be mailed to you. If you had petitioned for a name change, the judge may order the change at this time, and the certificate will reflect your new name. It is illegal to make photocopies of the naturalization document. Replacement certificates may be obtained by filing Form N-565. The naturalization certificate is the vehicle to acquire a U.S. passport, applications for which are now taken at most U.S. post offices.

CHAPTER 7

Children and War Veterans

A child born in the United States is automatically a U.S. citizen, regardless of the citizenship or immigration status of the parents. This is true even for children of illegal aliens or of unwed mothers.

Birth abroad to U.S. citizen

Children born abroad to U.S. citizen parents usually derive citizenship from their parents. There are some statutory requirements that such children must meet before they acquire U.S. citizenship. These requirements have changed over the years. Currently, a child acquires U.S. citizenship if both parents are citizens and at least one parent had lived in the United States at any time prior to the child's birth. The child also acquires citizenship if the parents are married but only one is a U.S. citizen, if the U.S. citizen parent had been physically present in the United States for at least five year's prior to the child's birth, at least two of which were after the parent turned 14.

Parents of children born abroad can apply for a Certificate of Citizenship (Form N-600) for their child. The certificate is simply a record or evidence of citizenship, much as a birth certificate is for children born in the United States. It does not confer citizenship, it is simply proof of it and makes it simpler to establish citizenship.

Children of unmarried couples

An illegitimate child of a U.S. citizen mother, if she had been physically present in the United States for at least one year at any time before the child's birth, is a U.S. citizen.

An illegitimate child born to a U.S. citizen father is also a U.S. citizen if the father had been present in the United States for at least one continuous year before the child's birth and had legitimated the child before the 18th birthday.

Adopted children

Adopted minor children of citizens acquire citizenship from their parents. Adoptive parents file form N-643 to document citizenship for their adopted children under the age of 18. Adopted children over 18 must file N-400 and meet the usual naturalization requirements listed in Chapter 3.

Derivative citizenship

Children below the age of 18 who are currently permanent residents are automatically naturalized if the other parent is a citizen or naturalizes at the same time. They do not have to meet either the language or the history and civics requirements. Minor children are also automatically naturalized with a parent, if the other parent is deceased or divorced or separated and the naturalizing parent has legal custody.

Unmarried children under 18, automatically become U.S. citizens when their parents naturalize under any of the following conditions:
- If the other parent is already a U.S. citizen;
- If both parents are naturalizing together;
- The mother is being naturalized and the child was born out of wedlock;
- The father is being naturalized, the child was born out of wedlock and the child was legitimated by the father before turning 16;
- The child's other parent is deceased;
- The parents are divorced or separated and the parent being naturalized has legal custody.

Petitioning

If your child does not automatically acquire citizenship at the time of your naturalization, you can file for a certificate of citizenship for the child. For instance if both spouses do not naturalize, you can apply for a Certificate of Citizenship (Form N-600) if the child is under 18 and is legally with you. Such certificates can be obtained if:
- At least one parent is a U.S. citizen by birth or naturalization;
- The child is physically and lawfully present in the United States;
- The child is under the age of 18 and in the legal custody of the citizen parent.

Veterans of U.S. Armed Forces

Individuals who have served in the U.S. Armed Forces are eligible to file for naturalization based on their current or prior U.S. military service. They should file the N-400 Military Naturalization Packet.

Applicants who have served for three years in the U.S. military and who are lawful permanent residents are excused from the residency and physical presence requirements if their applications for naturalization are filed while they are still serving or within six months of an honorable discharge. To be eligible for these exemptions, an applicant must:

- Have served honorably or separated under honorable conditions;
- Establish good moral character if service was discontinuous or not honorable;
- Completed three or more years of military service;
- Be a legal permanent resident at the time of the examination.

Applicants who file for naturalization after six months of a discharge can count their period of service toward the residence and physical presence requirements.

The continuous residence and physical presence requirements are also waived for veterans who have served honorably in the following wars:

- World War I: 4/16/17 to 11/11/18;
- World War II: 9/1/39 to 12/31/46;
- Korean: 6/25/50 to 7/1/55;
- Vietnam: 2/28/61 to 10/15/78;
- Operation Desert Shield/ Desert Storm: 8/29/90 to 4/11/91;
- Any other period, which the president, by executive order, has designated as a period in which the Armed Forces of the United States engaged in armed conflict with hostile foreign forces.

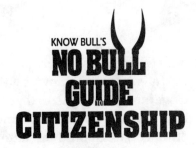

CHAPTER 8

Dual Citizenship

Even after you acquire U.S. citizen you may still retain your old citizenship, depending upon the laws of the country of your current citizenship. Countries define citizenship based on place of birth, descent, marriage, naturalization, etc. Since there are many ways to acquire citizenship, it is possible for someone to simultaneously be a citizen of two countries. Some countries are indifferent to the citizenship claims of other countries or forbid renunciation of their citizenship. Dual citizenship thus derives because of different laws governing citizenship among various countries.

The following is the official statement by the U.S. State Department on dual nationality:

Dual Nationality

The concept of dual nationality means that a person is a citizen of two countries at the same time. Each country has its own citizenship laws based on its own policy. Persons may have dual nationality by automatic operation of different laws rather than by choice. For example, a child born in a foreign country to U.S. citizen parents may be both a U.S. citizen and a citizen of the country of birth.

A U.S. citizen may acquire foreign citizenship by marriage, or a person naturalized as a U.S. citizen may not lose the citizenship of the country of birth. U.S. law does not mention dual nationality or require a person to choose one citizenship or another. Also, a person who is automatically granted another citizenship does not risk losing U.S. citizenship. However, a person who acquires a foreign citizenship by applying for it may lose U.S. citizenship. In order to lose U.S. citizenship, the law requires that the person must apply for the foreign citizenship voluntarily, by free choice, and with the intention to give up U.S. citizenship.

Intent can be shown by the person's statements or conduct. The U.S. Government recognizes that dual nationality exists but does not encourage it as a matter of policy because of the problems it may cause. Claims of other countries on dual national U.S. citizens may conflict with U.S. law, and dual nationality may limit U.S. Government efforts to assist citizens abroad. The country where a dual national is located generally has a stronger claim to that person's allegiance.

However, dual nationals owe allegiance to both the United States and the foreign country. They are required to obey the laws of both countries. Either country has the right to enforce its laws, particularly if the person later travels there. Most U.S. citizens, including dual nationals, must use a U.S. passport to enter and leave the United States. Dual nationals may also be required by the foreign country to use its passport to enter and leave that country. Use of the foreign passport does not endanger U.S. citizenship. Most countries permit a person to renounce or otherwise lose citizenship.

Information on losing foreign citizenship can be obtained from the foreign country's embassy and consulates in the United States. Americans can renounce U.S. citizenship in the proper form at U.S. embassies and consulates abroad.   — *Source: Department of State*

At your oath ceremony, you will be asked to renounce all foreign allegiances. Some countries may refuse to recognize your renunciation at the naturalization ceremony, however, and may continue to treat you as a citizen of their country, thereby bestowing you with dual nationality.

The question of dual nationality is determined by the nationality laws of your homeland. A citizen of Mexico, following a new nationality law adopted in March 1998, continues to retain Mexican citizenship even after naturalizing as a U.S. citizen. By contrast, citizens of India and China lose their citizenship if they accept the citizenship of another country. You are advised to contact your embassy or consulate to determine if you will retain dual citizenship after you take out U.S. citizenship.

Dual nationality is usually, though not always, advantageous. It could make you accountable to conflicting laws of two countries, which can be especially problematic when you are physically in the country. U.S. law permits you to retain a foreign passport, but your own country, if it permits dual nationality, may prohibit multiple passports. You are advised to check into the consequences of dual citizenship with your consulate. The following list identifies the consequences to your current citizenship after you take out U.S. citizenship, depending upon your current nationality:

Retain

You will retain your current citizenship even after you take out U.S. citizenship if you are a citizen of the following countries:

Albania	Ecuador	Nevis
Antigua	El Salvador	New Zealand
Argentina	Estonia	Nigeria
Barbados	France	Panama
Barbuda	Ghana	Peru
Belize	Greece	Poland
Benin	Grenada	Portugal
Brazil	Guatemala	Romania
Bulgaria	Hong Kong	Russia
Burkina Faso	Hungary	St. Christopher
Cambodia	Iran	and Nevis
Canada	Ireland	St. Kitts
Cape Verde	Israel	St. Lucia
Central African	Jamaica	Slovenia
Republic	Latvia	Sri Lanka
Colombia	Lesotho	Switzerland
Costa Rica	Liechtenstein	Syria
Cote D'Ivoire	Macao	Togo
Croatia	Maldives	Tunisia
Cyprus	Malta	Turkey
Dominica	Mexico	Tuvala
Dominican	Morocco	United Kingdom
Republic	Namibia	Uruguay

Lose

You will lose your current citizenship after you take out U.S. citizenship if you are a citizen of the following countries:

Algeria
Andorra
Australia
Austria
Azerbaijan
Bahrain
Belgium
Belarus
Bhutan
Bolivia
Botswana
Brunei
Burundi
Cameroon
Chile
China (People's
    Republic)
Czech Republic
Congo
Cuba
Denmark
Djibouti
Dominican Republic
Equatorial Guinea
Finland
Gabon
Germany
Guinea

Honduras
Iceland
India
Indonesia
Iraq
Italy
Japan
Kazakhstan
Kiribati
Korea
Kuwait
Kyrgyz Republic
Laos
Libya
Luxembourg
Malawi
Malaysia
Mali
Mongolia
Monaco
Myanmar (Burma)
Nepal
Netherlands
Nicaragua
Niger
North Korea
Norway
Oman

Pakistan
Palau
Papua New Guinea
Philippines
Principe
Qatar
Rwanda
Saudi Arabia
Singapore
Sierra Leone
Slovak Republic
South Africa
South Korea
Spain
Sri Lanka
Swaziland
Sweden
Sudan
Taiwan
Tonga
Uganda
Ukraine
United Arab
    Emirates
Uzbekistan
Venezuela
Yemen
Zimbabwe

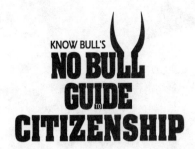

KNOW BULL'S
NO BULL GUIDE TO CITIZENSHIP

APPENDIX

Application for Naturalization
FORM N-400
FORM N-600

U.S. Department of Justice

Immigration and Naturalization Service

OMB #1115-0009

Application for Naturalization

INSTRUCTIONS

Purpose of This Form.
This form is for use to apply to become a naturalized citizen of the United States.

Who May File.
You may apply for naturalization if:

*   you have been a lawful permanent resident for five years;
*   you have been a lawful permanent resident for three years, have been married to a United States citizen for those three years, and continue to be married to that U.S. citizen;
*   you are the lawful permanent resident child of United States citizen parents; or
*   you have qualifying military service.

Children under 18 may automatically become citizens when their parents naturalize. You may inquire at your local Service office for further information. If you do not meet the qualifications listed above but believe that you are eligible for naturalization, you may inquire at your local Service office for additional information.

General Instructions.
Please answer all questions by typing or clearly printing in black ink. Indicate that an item is not applicable with "N/A". If an answer is "none," write "none". If you need extra space to answer any item, attach a sheet of paper with your name and your alien registration number (A#), if any, and indicate the number of the item.

Every application must be properly signed and filed with the correct fee. If you are under 18 years of age, your parent or guardian must sign the application.

If you wish to be called for your examination at the same time as another person who is also applying for naturalization, make your request on a separate cover sheet. Be sure to give the name and alien registration number of that person.

Initial Evidence Requirements.
You must file your application with the following evidence:

A copy of your alien registration card.

Photographs. You must submit two color photographs of yourself taken within 30 days of this application. These photos must be glossy, unretouched and unmounted, and have a white background. Dimension of the face should be about 1 inch from chin to top of hair. Face should be 3/4 frontal view of right side with right ear visible. Using pencil or felt pen, lightly print name and A#, if any, on the back of each photo. This requirement may be waived by the Service if you can establish that you are confined because of age or physical infirmity.

Form N-400 (Rev. 07/17/91)N / (Rev. 05/8/96)Y Fee change only Internet

Fingerprints. If you are between the ages of 14 and 75, you must submit your fingerprints on Form FD-258. Fill out the form and write your Alien Registration Number in the space marked "Your No. OCA" or "Miscellaneous No. MNU". Take the chart and these instructions to a police station, sheriff's office or an office of this Service, or other reputable person or organization for fingerprinting. (You should contact the police or sheriff's office before there since some of these offices do not take fingerprints for other government agencies.) You must sign the chart in the presence of the person taking your fingerprints and have that person sign his/her name, title, and the date in the space provided. Do not bend, fold, or crease the fingerprint chart.

U.S. Military Service. If you have ever served in the Armed Forces of the United States at any time, you must submit a completed Form G-325B. If your application is based on your military service you must also submit Form N-426, "Request for Certification of Military or Naval Service."

Application for Child. If this application is for a permanent resident child of U.S. citizen parents, you must also submit copies of the child's birth certificate, the parents' marriage certificate, and evidence of the parents' U.S. citizenship. If the parents are divorced, you must also submit the divorce decree and evidence that the citizen parent has legal custody of the child.

Where to File.
File this application at the local Service office having jurisdiction over your place of residence.

Fee.
The fee for this application is **$95.00.** The fee must be submitted in the exact amount. It cannot be refunded. **DO NOT MAIL CASH.**

All checks and money orders must be drawn on a bank or other institution located in the United States and must be payable in United States currency. The check or money order should be made payable to the Immigration and Naturalization Service, except that:

*   If you live in Guam, and are filing this application in Guam, make your check or money order payable to the "Treasurer, Guam."
*   If you live in the Virgin Islands, and are filing this application in the Virgin Islands, make your check or money order payable to the "Commissioner of Finance of the Virgin Islands."

Checks are accepted subject to collection. An uncollected check will render the application and any document issued invalid. A charge of $5.00 will be imposed if a check in payment of a fee is not honored by the bank on which it is drawn.

Processing Information.

Rejection. Any application that is not signed or is not accompanied by the proper fee will be rejected with a notice that the application is deficient. You may correct the deficiency and resubmit the application. However, an application is not considered properly filed until it is accepted by the Service.

Requests for more information. We may request more information or evidence. We may also request that you submit the originals of any copy. We will return these originals when they are no longer required.

Interview. After you file your application, you will be notified to appear at a Service office to be examined under oath or affirmation. This interview may not be waived. If you are an adult, you must show that you have a knowledge and understanding of the history, principles, and form of government of the United States. There is no exemption from this requirement.

You will also be examined on your ability to read, write, and speak English. If on the date of your examination you are more than 50 years of age and have been a lawful permanent resident for 20 years or more, or you are 55 years of age and have been a lawful permanent resident for at least 15 years, you will be exempt from the English language requirements of the law. If you are exempt, you may take the examination in any language you wish.

Oath of Allegiance. If your application is approved, you will be required to take the following oath of allegiance to the United States in order to become a citizen:

"I hereby declare, on oath, that I absolutely and entirely renounce and abjure all allegiance and fidelity to any foreign prince, potentate, state or sovereignty, of whom or which I have heretofore been a subject or citizen; that I will support and defend the Constitution and laws of the United States of America against all enemies, foreign and domestic; that I will bear true faith and allegiance to the same; that I will bear arms on behalf of the United States when required by the law; that I will perform noncombatant service in the armed forces of the United States when required by the law; that I will perform work of national importance under civilian direction when required by the law; and that I take this obligation freely without any mental reservation or purpose of evasion; so help me God."

If you cannot promise to bear arms or perform noncombatant service because of religious training and belief, you may omit those statements when taking the oath. "Religious training and belief" means a person's belief in relation to a Supreme Being involving duties superior to those arising from any human relation, but does not include essentially political, sociological, or philosophical views or merely a personal moral code.

Oath ceremony. You may choose to have the oath of allegiance administered in a ceremony conducted by the Service or request to be scheduled for an oath ceremony in a court that has jurisdiction over the applicant's place of residence. At the time of your examination you will be asked to elect either form of ceremony. You will become a citizen on the date of the oath ceremony and the Attorney General will issue a Certificate of Naturalization as evidence of United States citizenship.

If you wish to change your name as part of the naturalization process, you will have to take the oath in court.

Penalties.
If you knowingly and willfully falsify or conceal a material fact or submit a false document with this request, we will deny the benefit you are filing for, and may deny any other immigration benefit. In addition, you will face severe penalties provided by law, and may be subject to criminal prosecution.

Privacy Act Notice.
We ask for the information on this form, and associated evidence, to determine if you have established eligibility for the immigration benefit you are filing for. Our legal right to ask for this information is in 8 USC 1439, 1440, 1443, 1445, 1446, and 1452. We may provide this information to other government agencies. Failure to provide this information, and any requested evidence, may delay a final decision or result in denial of your request.

Paperwork Reduction Act Notice.
We try to create forms and instructions that are accurate, can be easily understood, and which impose the least possible burden on you to provide us with information. Often this is difficult because some immigration laws are very complex. Accordingly, the reporting burden for this collection of information is computed as follows: (1) learning about the law and form, 20 minutes; (2) completing the form, 25 minutes; and (3) assembling and filing the application (includes statutory required interview and travel time, after filing of application), 3 hours and 35 minutes, for an estimated average of 4 hours and 20 minutes per response. If you have comments regarding the accuracy of this estimate, or suggestions for making this form simpler, you can write to both the Immigration and Naturalization Service, 425 I Street, N.W., Room 5304, Washington, D.C. 20536; and the Office of Management and Budget, Paperwork Reduction Project, OMB No. 1115-0009, Washington, D.C. 20503.

U.S. Department of Justice
Immigration and Naturalization Service

OMB #1115-0009
Application for Naturalization

START HERE - Please Type or Print

Part 1.   Information about you.

Family Name	Given Name	Middle Initial

U.S. Mailing Address - Care of

Street Number and Name		Apt. #
City	County	
State	ZIP Code	

Date of Birth (month/day/year)	Country of Birth

Social Security #	A #

Part 2.   Basis for Eligibility *(check one).*

a. ☐ I have been a permanent resident for at least five (5) years .

b. ☐ I have been a permanent resident for at least three (3) years and have been married to a United States Citizen for those three years.

c. ☐ I am a permanent resident child of United States citizen parent(s) .

d. ☐ I am applying on the basis of qualifying military service in the Armed Forces of the U.S. and have attached completed Forms N-426 and G-325B

e. ☐ Other. (Please specify section of law)_____ .

Part 3.   Additional information about you.

Date you became a permanent resident (month/day/year)	Port admitted with an immmigrant visa or INS Office where granted adjustment of status.

Citizenship

Name on alien registration card (if different than in Part 1)

Other names used since you became a permanent resident (including maiden name)

Sex ☐ Male ☐ Female	Height	Marital Status: ☐ Single ☐ Divorced ☐ Married ☐ Widowed

Can you speak, read and write English ?   ☐No ☐Yes.

Absences from the U.S.:

Have you been absent from the U.S. since becoming a permanent resident?   ☐ No ☐Yes.

If you answered **"Yes"** , complete the following, Begin with your most recent absence. If you need more room to explain the reason for an absence or to list more trips, continue on separate paper.

Date left U.S.	Date returned	Did absence last 6 months or more?	Destination	Reason for trip
		Yes No		
		Yes No		
		Yes No		
		Yes No		
		Yes No		
		Yes No		

Form N-400 (Rev. 07/17/91)N Internet   *Continued on back.*

FOR INS USE ONLY

Returned	Receipt

Resubmitted

Reloc Sent

Reloc Rec'd

☐ Applicant Interviewed

At Interview

☐ request naturalization ceremony at court

Remarks

Action

To Be Completed by
Attorney or *Representative*, if any
Fill in box if G-28 is attached to represent the applicant

VOLAG#

ATTY State License #

Part 4. Information about your residences and employment.

A. List your addresses during the last five (5) years or since you became a permanent resident, whichever is less. Begin with your current address. If you need more space, continue on separate paper:

Street Number and Name, City, State, Country, and Zip Code	Dates (month/day/year)	
	From	To

B. List your employers during the last five (5) years. List your present or most recent employer first. If none, write "None". If you need more space, continue on separate paper.

Employer's Name	Employer's Address		Dates Employed (month/day/year)		Occupation/position
	Street Name and Number - City, State and ZIP Code		From	To	

Part 5. Information about your marital history.

A. Total number of times you have been married _____ . If you are now married, complete the following regarding your husband or wife.

Family name	Given name	Middle initial
Address		

Date of birth (month/day/year)	Country of birth	Citizenship
Social Security#	A# *(if applicable)*	Immigration status (If not a U.S. citizen)

Naturalization (If applicable)
(month/day/year)   Place   (City, State)

If you have ever previously been married or if your current spouse has been previously married, please provide the following on separate paper: Name of prior spouse, date of marriage, date marriage ended, how marriage ended and immigration status of prior spouse.

Part 6. Information about your children.

B. Total Number of Children _____ . Complete the following information for each of your children. If the child lives with you, state "with me" in the address column; otherwise give city/state/country of child's current residence. If deceased, write "deceased" in the address column.   If you need more space, continue on separate paper.

Full name of child	Date of birth	Country of birth	Citizenship	A - Number	Address

Continued on next page

◯   *Continued on back*   ◯

Part 7. Additional eligibility factors.

Please answer each of the following questions. If your answer is **"Yes"**, explain on a separate paper.

1. Are you now, or have you ever been a member of, or in any way connected or associated with the Communist Party, or ever knowingly aided or supported the Communist Party directly, or indirectly through another organization, group or person, or ever advocated, taught, believed in, or knowingly supported or furthered the interests of communism?   Yes   No

2. During the period March 23, 1933 to May 8, 1945, did you serve in, or were you in any way affiliated with, either directly or indirectly, any military unit, paramilitary unit, police unit, self-defense unit, vigilante unit, citizen unit of the Nazi party or SS, government agency or office, extermination camp, concentration camp, prisoner of war camp, prison, labor camp, detention camp or transit camp, under the control or affiliated with:

    a. The Nazi Government of Germany?   Yes   No

    b. Any government in any area occupied by, allied with, or established with the assistance or cooperation of, the Nazi Government of Germany?   Yes   No

3. Have you at any time, anywhere, ever ordered, incited, assisted, or otherwise participated in the persecution of any person because of race, religion, national origin, or political opinion?   Yes   No

4. Have you ever left the United States to avoid being drafted into the U.S. Armed Forces?   Yes   No

5. Have you ever failed to comply with Selective Service laws?   Yes   No

    If you have registered under the Selective Service laws, complete the following information:

        Selective Service Number:_____   Date Registered:_____

    If you registered before 1978, also provide the following:

        Local Board Number:_____   Classification:_____

6. Did you ever apply for exemption from military service because of alienage, conscientious objections or other reasons?   Yes   No

7. Have you ever deserted from the military, air or naval forces of the United States?   Yes   No

8. Since becoming a permanent resident , have you ever failed to file a federal income tax return ?   Yes   No

9. Since becoming a permanent resident , have you filed a federal income tax return as a nonresident or failed to file a federal return because you considered yourself to be a nonresident?   Yes   No

10 Are deportation proceedings pending against you, or have you ever been deported, or ordered deported, or have you ever applied for suspension of deportation?   Yes   No

11. Have you ever claimed in writing, or in any way, to be a United States citizen?   Yes   No

12. Have you ever:

    a. been a habitual drunkard?   Yes   No

    b. advocated or practiced polygamy?   Yes   No

    c. been a prostitute or procured anyone for prostitution?   Yes   No

    d. knowingly and for gain helped any alien to enter the U.S. illegally?   Yes   No

    e. been an illicit trafficker in narcotic drugs or marijuana?   Yes   No

    f. received income from illegal gambling?   Yes   No

    g. given false testimony for the purpose of obtaining any immigration benefit?   Yes   No

13. Have you ever been declared legally incompetent or have you ever been confined as a patient in a mental institution?   Yes   No

14. Were you born with, or have you acquired in same way, any title or order of nobility in any foreign State?   Yes   No

15. Have you ever:

    a. knowingly committed any crime for which you have not been arrested?   Yes   No

    b. been arrested, cited, charged, indicted, convicted, fined or imprisoned for breaking or violating any law or ordinance excluding traffic regulations?   Yes   No

(If you answer yes to 15 , in your explanation give the following information for each incident or occurrence the **city**, **state**, and **country**, where the offense took place, the **date** and **nature** of the offense, and the **outcome** or **disposition** of the case).

Part 8. Allegiance to the U.S.

If your answer to any of the following questions is **"NO"**, attach a full explanation:

    1. Do you believe in the Constitution and form of government of the U.S.?   Yes   No

    2. Are you willing to take the full Oath of Allegiance to the U.S.? (see instructions)   Yes   No

    3. If the law requires it, are you willing to bear arms on behalf of the U.S.?   Yes   No

    4. If the law requires it, are you willing to perform noncombatant services in the Armed Forces of the U.S.?   Yes   No

    5. If the law requires it, are you willing to perform work of national importance under civilian direction?   Yes   No

Part 9. Memberships and organizations.

A. List your present and past membership in or affiliation with every organization, association, fund, foundation, party, club, society, or similar group in the United States or in any other place. Include any military service in this part. If none, write "none". Include the name of organization, location, dates of membership and the nature of the organization. If additional space is needed, use separate paper.

_____

_____

_____

Part 10. Complete only if you checked block " C " in Part 2.

How many of your parents are U.S. citizens?   One   Both   (Give the following about one U.S. citizen parent:)

Family Name	Given Name	Middle Name

Address

Basis for citizenship: Birth Naturalization Cert. No.	Relationship to you (check one): natural parent adoptive parent parent of child legitimated after birth

If adopted or legitimated after birth, give date of adoption or, legitimation: (month/day/year)_____.

Does this parent have legal custody of you?   Yes   No

(Attach a copy of relating evidence to establish that you are the child of this U.S. citizen and evidence of this parent's citizenship.)

Part 11. Signature.   (Read the information on penalties in the instructions before completing this section).

I certify or, if outside the United States, I swear or affirm, under penalty of perjury under the laws of the United States of America that this application, and the evidence submitted with it, is all true and correct. I authorize the release of any information from my records which the Immigration and Naturalization Service needs to determine eligibility for the benefit I am seeking.

Signature   **Date**

Please Note: If you do not completely fill out this form, or fail to submit required documents listed in the instructions, you may not be found eligible for naturalization and this application may be denied.

Part 12. Signature of person preparing form if other than above. *(Sign below)*

I declare that I prepared this application at the request of the above person and it is based on all information of which I have knowledge.

Signature   **Print Your Name**   **Date**

Firm Name
and Address

DO NOT COMPLETE THE FOLLOWING UNTIL INSTRUCTED TO DO SO AT THE INTERVIEW

I swear that I know the contents of this application, and supplemental pages   1 through____, that the corrections , numbered 1 through____, were made at my request, and that this amended application, is true to the best of my knowledge and belief.

Subscribed and sworn to before me by the applicant.

_____
(Examiner's Signature)   Date

_____
(Complete and true signature of applicant)

U.S. Department of Justice
Immigration and Naturalization Service

**APPLICATION FOR CERTIFICATE OF
CITIZENSHIP**

INSTRUCTIONS
(Tear off this instruction sheet before filling out this form)

This form is not for children adopted by United States Citizens. It may be used for children adopted by alien parents who were later naturalized. It must be completely filled in. Print the answers in ink or use typewriter. If you do not have enough room for any answer or if the instructions tell you to use a separate sheet of paper, use another sheet this size, giving the answer the same number as the number of the question, and attach it to the application. You will later be notified to appear for examination before an officer of the Immigration and Naturalization Service. You may be requested to bring a relative or other witness to provide additional testimony.

AGE OF APPLICANT - Applicants 14 years of age or over must sign their full names, but only in the space provided on page 3 of this application. If under 14 years, only the parent or guardian must sign his or her name and only in the space provided on page 3.

FEE - A fee of ninety dollars ($90) must be paid for filing this application. It cannot be refunded regardless of the action taken on the application. DO NOT MAIL CASH. ALL FEES MUST BE SUBMITTED IN THE EXACT AMOUNT. Payment by check or money order must be drawn on a bank or other institution located in United States and be payable in United States currency. If applicant resides in Guam, check or money order must be payable to the "Treasurer Guam." If applicant resides in the Virgin Islands, check or money order must be payable to the "Commissioner of Finance of the Virgin Islands." All other applicants must make the check or money order payable to the "Immigration and Naturalization Service." When check is drawn on account of a person other than the applicant, the name of the applicant must be entered on the face of the check. If application is submitted from outside the United States, remittance may be made by bank international money order or foreign draft drawn on a financial institution in the United States and payable to the Immigration and Naturalization Service in United States currency. Personal checks are accepted subject to collectibility. An uncollectible check will render the application and any document issued pursuant thereto invalid. A charge of $5.00 will be imposed if a check in payment of a fee is not honored by the bank on which it is drawn.

PHOTOGRAPHS - You are required to send with this application three identical unglazed photographs of yourself taken within 30 days of the date of this application. These photographs must be 2 x 2 inches in size and the distance from top of head to point of chin should be approximately 1 1/4 inches; must *not* be pasted on a card or mounted in any other way; must be on thin paper, have a light background, and clearly show a front view of your face without hat. Snapshots, groups, or full - length portraits or machine - made photographs will not be accepted. YOUR PHOTOGRAPHS MUST NOT BE SIGNED, but you should print your name and alien registration number, if any, in the center of the *back* of each photograph lightly with a soft lead pencil, taking care not to mutilate the photograph. They may be in natural color or in black and white, but black and white photographs which have been tinted or otherwise colored are not acceptable.

FACTS CONCERNING ARRIVAL IN THE UNITED STATES - Detailed information should be given in Statement 3 regarding your first arrival in the United States for permanent residence in this country. The information regarding the number of the passport and date and place of issuance does not need to be given unless you traveled on a *United States* passport at that time. If you do not know the exact date of arrival or name of the vessel or port and cannot obtain this information, give the facts of your arrival to the best of your ability. If you have an alien registration receipt card, immigrant identification card, ship's card, or baggage labels, they will help you to give this information.

NAME TO BE SHOWN ON CERTIFICATE - The certificate will be issued only in a name that you have a legal right to use.

DOCUMENTS - If your birth abroad, or the birth abroad of any person through whom citizenship is claimed, was registered with an American Consul there, submit with this application any registration form that was issued. If any required documents were submitted to and **RETAINED by the American Consul in connection with such registration, or in connection with the issuance of a United States passport or in any other official matter, and you wish to use such documents in connection with this application instead of submitting duplicate copies, merely list the documents in Statement 14 of the application and give the location of the Consulate.** If you wish to make similar use of required documents contained in any Immigration and Naturalization Service file, list them in Statement 14 and identify the file by name, number, and location. Otherwise, the documents as mentioned in the box on page 6 applicable to your case (see over) must accompany your application and, for any required document not furnished, you must explain why; what efforts you have made to get it; and, if possible, enclose a statement from the official custodian of such records showing that the document is not available. You should also forward for consideration, in lieu of that document, a record or the affidavits described under **SECONDARY EVIDENCE**, on the reverse of this page.

If any person through whom citizenship is claimed became a citizen through his or her parent(s), but does not have a certificate of citizenship (with a number preceded by an A or AA) in his or her own name, communicate with the Immigration and Naturalization Service for information as to additional documents which must be submitted.

Form N - 600 (Rev. 04/11/91) Y

INSTRUCTIONS (Continued)

Any document in a foreign language must be accompanied by a translation in English. The translator must certify that he/she is competent to translate and that the translation is accurate. Do not send a Certificate of Naturalization or Citizenship and do not make any copy of such a certificate. An interview in connection with your application will be scheduled before an officer of the Immigration and Naturalization Service, and any Certificate of Naturalization or Citizenship may be presented in person at that time. If the law does not prohibit the making of copies send in a legible copy of any document which you submit with the application, but bring the original of any submitted copy with you to the interview. The original will be returned to you and the copy retained. You may be called upon to present proof of a parent's residence or physical presence in the United States.

IF CLAIMING CITIZENSHIP THROUGH FATHER (OR BOTH PARENTS)

1. Applicant's birth certificate.
2. Marriage certificate of applicant's parents.
3. If applicant's parents were married before their marriage to each other, death certificate or divorce decree showing the termination of any previous marriage of each parent.
4. If applicant is a woman and has ever been married, her marriage certificate(s).
5. If applicant's parent(s) became citizen(s) at birth, birth certificate(s) of parent(s).
6. Death certificate(s) of applicant's parent(s), if deceased.
7. If applicant is an adopted child, applicant's adoption decree.

IF CLAIMING CITIZENSHIP THROUGH MOTHER

1. Applicant's birth certificate.
2. Marriage certificate(s) of applicant's mother.
3. If applicant is a woman and has ever been married, her marriage certificate(s).
4. If applicant's mother became a citizen of the United States at birth, mother's birth certificate.
5. If applicant is claiming citizenship through mother's marriage before September 22, 1922, to applicant's stepfather, death certificate or divorce decree showing termination of any previous marriage(s) of mother and stepfather.
6. If applicant is claiming citizenship through mother's marriage before September 22, 1922, to applicant's stepfather and stepfather became a citizen of the united States at birth, stepfather's birth certificate.
7. Death certificate of applicant's mother, if deceased.

IF CLAIMING CITIZENSHIP THROUGH HUSBAND
(NOTE: APPLICABLE ONLY IF MARRIAGE OCCURRED PRIOR TO SEPTEMBER 22, 1922.)

1. If husband through whom citizenship is claimed became a citizen of the United States at birth, husband's birth certificate.
2. Applicant's marriage certificate(s).
3. If either applicant or the husband through whom she is claiming citizenship was married before their marriage to each other, death certificate or divorce decree showing the termination of each such prior marriage(s).
4. If applicant's marriage to the husband through whom she is claiming citizenship has terminated, death certificate or divorce decree showing such a termination.

SECONDARY EVIDENCE

If it is not possible to obtain any one of the required documents or records shown above, the following may be submitted for consideration:

1. *Baptismal certificate.* - A certificate under the seal of the church where the baptism occurred, showing date and place of the child's birth, date of baptism, the names of the godparents, if known.
2. *School record.* - A letter from the school authorities having jurisdiction over school attended (preferably the first school), showing the date of admission to the school, child's date of birth or age at that time, place of birth, and the names and places of birth of parents, if shown in the school records.
3. *Census record.*- State or Federal census record showing the name(s) and place(s) of birth, and date(s) of birth or age(s) of the person(s) listed.
4. *Affidavits.*- Notarized affidavits of two persons who were living at the time, and who have personal knowledge, of the event you are trying to prove - for example, the date and place of a birth, marriage, or death. The persons making the affidavits may be relatives and need not be citizens of the United States. Each affidavit should contain the following information regarding the person making the affidavit: His (Her) full name and address; date and place of birth; relationship to you, if any; full information concerning the event; and complete details concerning how he (she) acquired knowledge of the event.

U.S. DEPARTMENT OF JUSTICE
IMMIGRATION AND NATURALIZATION SERVICE

APPLICATION FOR CERTIFICATE OF CITIZENSHIP

OMB No. 1115-0018

FEE STAMP

Date _____

Take or mail this application to:
IMMIGRATION AND NATURALIZATION SERVICE

(Print or type) _____ nee _____
         (Full, True Name, without Abbreviations)   (Maiden name, if any)

_____
(Apartment number, Street address, and if appropriate, "in care of")

_____
(City)   (Country)   (State)   (ZIP Code)

_____
(Telephone Number)

ALIEN REGISTRATION

No. _____

(SEE INSTRUCTIONS. BE SURE YOU UNDERSTAND EACH QUESTION BEFORE YOU ANSWER IT.)

I hereby apply to the Commissioner of Immigration and Naturalization for a certificate showing that I am a citizen of the United States of America.

(1) I was born in _____ on _____
         (City) (State or Country)   (Month) (Day) (Year)

(2) My personal description is: Sex _____ ; complexion _____ ; color of eyes _____ ; color of hair _____ ; height ____ feet ____ inches;

weight _____ pounds; visible distinctive marks _____

Marital status: ☐ Single;   ☐ Married;   ☐ Divorced;   ☐ Widow(er).

(3) I arrived in the United States at _____ on _____
         (City and State)   (Month) (Day) (Year)

under the name _____ by means of _____
                         (Name of ship or other means of arrival)

☐ on U. S. Passport No. _____ issued to me at _____ on _____
                                        (Month) (Day) (Year)

☐ on an Immigrant Visa.   ☐ Other (specify)_____

---

(4) FILL IN THIS BLOCK ONLY IF YOU ARRIVED IN THE UNITED STATES BEFORE JULY 1, 1924.

(a) My last permanent foreign residence was _____
                                    (City)   (Country)

(b) I took the ship or other conveyance to the United States at _____
                                    (City)   (Country)

(c) I was coming to _____ at _____
         (Name of person in the United States)   (City and State where this person was living)

(d) I traveled to the United States with _____
                     (Names of passengers or relatives with whom you traveled, and their relationship to you, if any)

(5) Have you been out of the United States since you first arrived? ☐Yes ☐No; If "Yes" fill in the following information for every absence.

DATE DEPARTED	DATE RETURNED	Name Of Airlines Or Other Means Used To Return To The United States	Port Of Return To The United States

(6) I_____ filed a petition for naturalization. (*If* "have" *attach full explanation.*)
    (have) (have not)

TO THE APPLICANT. - Do not write between the double lines below. Continue on next page.

ARRIVAL RECORDS EXAMINED	ARRIVAL RECORD FOUND
Card index _____	Place _____ Date _____
Index books _____	Name _____
Manifests _____	Manner _____
_____	Marital status _____ Age_____
	(Signature of person making search)

Form N-600 (Rev. 04/11/91)Y   (1)   ☆ U.S. Government Printing Office 1993-362-409

(CONTINUE HERE)

(7) **I claim United States citizenship through my** *(check whichever applicable)* ❑ **father;** ❑ **mother;** ❑ **both parents;**

❑ **adoptive parent(s)** ❑ **husband**

(8) **My father's name is** _____ ; he was born on _____

    (Month)   (Day)   (Year)

at _____ ; and resides at _____

   (City)   (State or Country)   (Street address, city and State or country. If dead, write

_____He became a citizen of the United States by ❑ birth; ❑ naturalization on _____

"dead" and date of death.)   (Month)   (Day)   (Year)

in the _____Certificate of Naturalization No. _____;

        (Name of court, city and State)

❑ through his parent(s), and _____ **issued Certificate of Citizenship No. A or AA** _____

                              (was)   (was not)

(If known) His former Alien Registration No. was _____

He _____lost United States citizenship. (*If citizenship lost, attach full explanation.*)

   (has)   (has not)

He resided in the United States from _____ to _____ ; from _____ to _____ ; from _____ to _____ ;

                                    (Year)   (Year)   (Year)   (Year)   (Year)   (Year)

from _____ to _____ ; from _____ to _____ ; I am the child of his _____ marriage.

      (Year)   (Year)   (Year)   (Year)   (1st, 2d, 3d, etc.)

(9) **My mother's present name is** _____ ; her maiden name was _____ ;

she was born on _____ ; at _____ ; she resides

                (Month) (Day) (Year)   (City) (State or country)

at _____ She became a citizen of the

   (Street address, city, and State or country. If dead write "dead" and date of death.)

United States by ❑ birth; ❑ naturalization under the name of _____

on _____ in the _____

   (Month) (Day) (Year)   (Name of court, city, and State)

Certificate of Naturalization No. _____ ; ❑ through her parent(s), and _____ issued Certificate of

                                                                                    (was)   (was not)

Citizenship No. A or AA _____ (If known) Her former Alien Registration No. was _____

She _____ lost United States citizenship. (*If citizenship lost, attach full explanation.*)

    (has)   (has not)

She resided in the United States from _____ to _____ ; from _____ to _____ ; from _____ to _____ ;

                                     (Year)   (Year)   (Year)   (Year)   (Year)   (Year)

from _____ to _____ ; from _____ to _____ ; I am the child of her _____ marriage.

      (Year)   (Year)   (Year)   (Year)   (1st, 2d, 3d, etc.)

(10) My mother and my father were married to each other on _____ at _____

                                                          (Month) (Day) (Year)   (City)   (State or country)

(11) If claim is through adoptive parent(s):

I was adopted on _____ in the _____

                (Month) (Day) (Year)   (Name of Court)

at _____by my _____ who were not United States citizens at that time.

   (city or town) (State) (Country)   (mother, father, parents)

(12) My _____ served in the Armed Forces of the United States from _____ to _____ and _____

       (father)   (mother)   (Date)   (Date)   (was) (was not)

honorably discharged.

(13) I _____ lost my United States citizenship. (*If citizenship lost, attach full explanation.*)

      (have)   (have not)

(14) I submit the following documents with this application:

Nature of Document	*Names of Persons Concerned*
_____	_____
_____	_____
_____	_____
_____	_____
_____	_____

(15) Fill in this block if your brother, sister, mother or father ever applied to the Immigration Service for a certificate of citizenship.

NAME OF RELATIVE	RELATIONSHIP	Date of Birth	WHEN APPLICATION SUBMITTED	CERTIFICATE NO. AND FILE NO., IF KNOWN, AND LOCATION OF OFFICE

(16) Fill in this block only if you are now or ever have been a married woman. I have been married _____ time(s), as follows:
(1, 2, 3, etc.)

DATE MARRIED	NAME OF HUSBAND	CITIZENSHIP OF HUSBAND	IF MARRIAGE HAS BEEN TERMINATED: Date Marriage Ended	How Marriage Ended (Death or Divorce)

(17) Fill in this block only if you claim citizenship through a husband. (*Marriage must have occurred prior to September 22, 1922.*)

Name of citizen husband _____ (Give full and complete name) ; he was born on _____ (Month) (Day) (Year)

at _____ (City) (State or country) ; and resides at _____ (Street address, city, and State or country. If dead, write "dead" and date of death.) He became a citizen of the

United States by ☐ birth; ☐ naturalization on _____ (Month) (Day) (Year) in the _____ (Name of court, city, and State) Certificate of

Naturalization No. _____ ; ☐ through his parent(s), and _____ (was) (was not) issued Certificate of

Citizenship No. A or AA _____ He _____ (has) (has not) since lost United States citizenship. (*If citizenship lost, attach full explanation.*)

I am of the _____ race. Before my marriage to him, he was married _____ (1, 2, 3, etc.) time(s), as follows:

DATE MARRIED	NAME OF WIFE	IF MARRIAGE HAS BEEN TERMINATED: Date Marriage Ended	How Marriage Ended (Death or Divorce)

(18) Fill in this block only if you claim citizenship through your stepfather. (*Applicable only if mother married U.S.Citizen prior to September 22, 1922.*)

The full name of my stepfather is _____ ; he was born on _____ (Month) (Day) (Year) at _____ (City) (State or country);

and resides at _____ (Street address, city, and State or country. If dead, write "dead" and date of death.) He became a citizen of the United States by ☐ birth;

☐ naturalization on _____ (Month) (Day) (Year) in the _____ (Name of court, city and State) Certificate of Naturalization No. _____ ;

☐ through his parent(s), and _____ (was) (was not) issued Certificate of Citizenship No. A or AA _____ He _____ (has) (has not) since lost United

States citizenship. (*If citizenship lost, attach full explanation.*) He and my mother were married to each other on _____ (Month) (Day) (Year) at _____ (City and State or

country) My mother is of the _____ race. She _____ (was) (was not) issued Certificate of Citizenship No. A _____

Before marrying my mother, my stepfather was married _____ (1, 2, 3, etc.) time(s), as follows:

DATE MARRIED	NAME OF WIFE	IF MARRIAGE HAS BEEN TERMINATED: Date Marriage Ended	How Marriage Ended (Death or Divorce)

(19) I _____ (have) (have not) previously applied for a certificate of citizenship on _____ (Date) , at _____ (Office)

(20) Signature of person preparing form. If other than applicant. I declare that this document was prepared by me at the request of the applicant and is based on all information of which I have any knowledge.

SIGNATURE:

ADDRESS: _____ DATE: _____

(SIGN HERE) _____
(Signature of applicant or parent or guardian)

(3)

APPLICANT. - Do not fill in or sign anything on this page

AFFIDAVIT

I, the _____ , do swear
(Applicant, parent, guardian)
that I know and understand the contents of this application, signed by me,
and of attached supplementary pages numbered (   ) to (   ), inclusive; that
the same are true to the best of my knowledge and belief; and that
corrections numbered (   ) to (   ) were made by me or at my request.

Subscribed and sworn to before me upon examination of the applicant
(parent, guardian) at _____ ,
this _____ day of _____ , 19 _____
and continued solely for:

_____
(Signature of applicant, parent, guardian)

_____
(Officer's Signature and Title)

REPORT AND RECOMMENDATION ON APPLICATION

On the basis of the documents, records, and persons examined, and the identification upon personal appearance of the underage beneficiary, I find that
all the facts and conclusions set forth under oath in this application are _____ true and correct; that the applicant did _____ derive or acquire United
States citizenship on _____ , through
(Month) (Day) (Year)

and that (s)he _____ been expatriated since that time. I recommend that this application be _____ and that
(has) (has not)   (granted)   (denied)
_____ Certificate of citizenship be _____ issued in the name of _____
(A)   (AA)
In addition to the documents listed in Item 14, the following documents and records have been examined:

Person Examined	Address	Relationship to Applicant	Date Testimony Heard
_____	_____	_____	_____
_____	_____	_____	_____
_____	_____	_____	_____

Supplementary Report(s) No.(s) _____ Attached.
Date _____ , 19 _____

_____
(Officer's Signature and Title)

I do _____ concur in the recommendation

Date _____ , 19 _____

_____
(Signature of District Director or Officer in Charge)

(4)

FROM THOSE WHO
KNOW BULL

FOR THOSE WHO
WOULD RATHER NOT

KNOW BULL'S
NO BULL
GUIDES

F E E D B A C K   C A R D

To get on our mailing list for announcements about new titles, propose new titles, or to suggest ways to take any bull out of this book, mail this form, or a copy, today!

NAME DINO PLEVRITES DATE

ADDRESS 333 E 79 NEW YORK

PHONE 4899320

CITY   STATE   ZIP 10021

WHERE DID HEAR ABOUT THIS BOOK?

WHERE DID YOU PURCHASE THIS BOOK?

HOW HELPFUL WAS THIS BOOK?   (NO BULL)   5   4   3   2   1   (ALL BULL)

SUGGESTIONS FOR IMPROVING THIS BOOK

WHAT OTHER SUBJECT WOULD YOU LIKE?

MAIL TO: NOBLE PUBLISHERS, 101 N 5TH STREET #310, READING, PA 19601